BTEC National

Health &
Social Care

BTEC National
Health & Social Care
Textbook & CD-ROM

Elizabeth Rasheed, Alison Hetherington, Linda Wyatt

Hodder Arnold

A MEMBER OF THE HODDER HEADLINE GROUP

This material has been endorsed by Edexcel and offers high quality support for the delivery of Edexcel qualifications. Edexcel endorsement does not mean that this material is essential to achieve any Edexcel qualification, nor does it mean that this is the only suitable material available to support any Edexcel qualification. No endorsed material will be used verbatim in setting any Edexcel examination and any resource lists produced by Edexcel shall include this and other appropriate texts. While this material has been through an Edexcel quality assurance process, all responsibility for the content remains with the publisher. Copies of official specifications for all Edexcel qualifications may be found on the Edexcel website – www.edexcel.org.uk

THE SHEFFIELD COLLEGE
CASTLE COLLEGE

600006915I	
Coutts	29/4/08
362	£21-99
MAY 2008	REF

Orders: please contact Bookpoint Ltd, 130 Milton Park, Abingdon, Oxon OX14 4SB. Telephone: (44) 01235 827720. Fax: (44) 01235 400454. Lines are open from 9.00–5.00, Monday to Saturday, with a 24 hour message answering service. You can also order through our website www.hoddereducation.co.uk.

British Library Cataloguing in Publication Data
A catalogue record for this title is available from the British Library

ISBN: 978 0 340 95862 9

First Published 2007
Impression number   10 9 8 7 6 5 4 3 2 1
Year   2012 2011 2010 2009 2008 2007

Copyright © 2007 Elizabeth Rasheed, Alison Hetherington, Linda Wyatt

All rights reserved. No part of this publication may be reproduced or transmitted in any form or by any means, electronic or mechanical, including photocopy, recording, or any information storage and retrieval system, without permission in writing from the publisher or under licence from the Copyright Licensing Agency Limited. Further details of such licences (for reprographic reproduction) may be obtained from the Copyright Licensing Agency Limited, Saffron House, 6–10 Kirby Street, London EC1N 8TS.

Cover photo © Richard T. Nowitz/Corbis
Typeset by Fakenham Photosetting Ltd, Fakenham, Norfolk
Printed in Italy for Hodder Arnold, an imprint of Hodder Education and a member of the Hodder Headline Group, an Hachette Livre UK company, 338 Euston Road, London NW1 3BH

Contents

Acknowledgements

I would like to thank my husband and children for their patience and support while I contributed to this book. I would also like to thank the staff I work with for their professional approach to maintaining the standards in health and social care education.

Liz Rasheed

I would like to thank my husband John for his support and my daughters Laura and Sally for their technical help and advice. Also my good friend Alison for her encouragement and advice. I would also like to thank my work colleagues at Mid Cheshire College for their support during the time I have spent researching and contributing to this exciting new book.

Alison Hetherington

I would like to thank my friends who have listened to me, made me many cups of tea and cooked dinner during the writing of this book, especially Kate, Nik, Harriet, Clair, Andy CP, Andy V, Jez, and the DH'ers, especially Jo, Carmel and Ruth. Thanks are also due to my colleagues Kim and Maggie for their support. Lastly, I would like to acknowledge and thank Mike, Angela, Will and my parents for their continual love, support and encouragement.

Linda Wyatt

The authors and publishers would like to thank the following for the use of photographs in this volume:

In the book: p.17 (left) © Zero-Gravity Corporation/handout/epa/Corbis; p.17 (right) Doug Peters/EMPICS Entertainment/PA Photos; p.19 (all) Stockdisc/Getty Images; p.28 Photo reproduced by kind permission of Doreen Lawrence, Director of The Stephen Lawrence Trust; p.31 FoodPix/Jupiter Images; p.52 http://www.hse-books.com/Books/product/image.asp? catalog%5Fname=HSEBooks&product%5Fid=2407/ Reproduced under the terms of the Click-Use License; p.67 Department of Clinical Radiology, Salisbury District Hospital/Science Photo Library; p.72 GustoImages/Science Photo Library; p.81 Russell D. Curtis/Science Photo Library; p.85 Lauren Shear/Science Photo Library; p.110 (left) © Phototake Inc./Alamy; p.110 (right) Innerspace Imaging/Science Photo Library; p.155 © Malcolm Brice/Photofusion; p.182 © Popperfoto/Alamy; p.187 Paul Fievez/BIPs/Getty Images; p.197 © ML Sinibaldi/Corbis; p.198 © Bettmann/Corbis; p.199 Omikron/Science Photo Library; p.208 © Phototake Inc./Alamy.

On CD-ROM: Unit 20, p.2 © Robert Estall photo agency/Alamy; p.5 Department for Transport Publications Centre/Reproduced under the terms of the Click-Use License; p.17 British Heart Foundation; Unit 22, p.3 © Crispin Rodwell/Alamy; p.6 Topfoto.co.uk; p.9 © Popperfoto/Alamy; p.12 Neil Harding/ Getty Images; Unit 29, p.2 © Michael Kemter/iStockphoto.com; p.3 Photodisc; p.13 Great Ape Trust of Iowa; p.14 © Albert Bandura; p.17 Martin Rogers/Getty Images; p.28 Michael Wintersgill/Scottish Viewpoint.

Every effort has been made to trace and acknowledge ownership of copyright. The publishers will be glad to make suitable arrangements with any copyright holders whom it has not been possible to contact.

Introduction

We are teachers as well as vocational specialists and we value the BTEC approach, which combines theory with practice. If you are new to BTEC, either as a student or as a teacher, we hope you find this book helpful, interesting and a useful introduction to this vocational area. It is a distillation of our experience of teaching in health and social care but no one has all the answers. We would appreciate feedback and suggestions for improvement which we may incorporate into later editions.

Note for students – this is a textbook. Dip into it. Use it. Discuss it. Don't try to read it from cover to cover like a novel and please don't copy chunks out of it!

The eight chapters in this book cover the core units for BTEC National in Health & Social Care. In addition, you will find a CD-ROM at the back of this book which covers the six most popular optional units.

> Remember, you should always respect the dignity and privacy of others when discussing placements, service users, or other health & social care experiences. When describing actual events, people, or settings, always keep names and identities anonymous.

Developing Effective Communication in Health and Social Care

Good communication skills are vital for those working in social work, nursing, occupational therapy or many of the other professions in health and social care.

This unit helps you to develop effective skills for interaction and communication. You are encouraged to examine factors that help or hinder communication and to look at what makes interpersonal skills effective in a work-related situation. You will reflect on your own performance and that of others. Communication is an essential skill to develop in preparation for work experience, and you may find that placement gives opportunities for some of the assessment of the unit.

Learning Outcomes

On completion of this unit you should be able to:

1 Understand effective communication and interpersonal interaction
2 Understand factors that influence communication and interpersonal interactions in health and social care settings
3 Know how patients/service users may be assisted by effective communication
4 Be able to demonstrate own communication skills in a caring role

1 Understand effective communication and interpersonal interaction

KEY CONCEPTS

Communication implies an exchange of ideas. It is a two-way process.

Activity 1

Make a list or mind map of all the ways you have communicated with someone today.
Now compare your list with another person's list.

Perhaps your list for Activity 1 includes some of these:

- Talking with friends in a group while waiting for class
- Talking to a patient or relative
- Making a formal presentation in class
- Reading or writing an assignment
- Looking at a picture and thinking about the meaning of it

- Listening to music
- Producing a poster
- Word processing an assignment
- Sending an e-mail
- Mobile phone conversation

These are all types of communication we use every day.

For P1, see whether you can identify which type of communication you have used in placement with service users, relatives or other workers. Complete the grid in Activity 2 by putting your activity in the second column.

Activity 2

TYPE OF COMMUNICATION	YOUR EXAMPLE
One-to-one	
Groups	
Formal	
Informal	
Written text	
Oral	
Visual	
Touch	
Music and drama	
Arts and crafts	
Using technology	

Remember

Communication involves interaction between people. The people do not have to be physically present – for example, you listen to a favourite song; the singer is not there but you hear the message and respond emotionally to the words, so communication has occurred. You may see a picture and respond to the message.

Types of interpersonal interaction

When you meet 'jargon', break it down into words you can understand. 'Inter' means between, so 'interpersonal' means between people. Interaction is action between people.

Here are some types of interpersonal interaction you may have used today:

- Speech – what words have you exchanged with people today?
- Language such as dialect, slang or jargon – do you use words with your friends or family that you do not use with others?
- Non-verbal interaction – did you smile? Did you shrug your shoulders? Did you turn your back on someone? Your posture, your facial expressions all convey meaning which people interpret. A touch can convey sympathy. Silence can be disapproving or supportive according to the facial expression that accompanies it.

Activity 3

- Think of someone you are fond of. How physically close do you get to them?
- Now think of someone you do not like. How physically close do you get to them?
- Is there a difference between the first and the second?

Personal space or physical nearness varies among individuals. Some people like to keep a distance between themselves and others; some people feel comfortable when close.

People vary in how much personal space they like. In some cultures people in conversation may stand close. In other cultures, people prefer a greater distance between them and another person.

Listening is part of the communication cycle. To listen implies that the listener hears *and* pays attention. Reflecting back is a good way to check that you have really listened. Use terms such as 'so are you saying...?' to check you have understood the other person.

The communication cycle can be applied to any communication situation.

- Idea occurs – shall we go out at the weekend?
- Message coded – into written words on a note or text on a mobile phone or spoken word
- Message sent – note or text sent to recipient or spoken to recipient
- Message received – note read by recipient or text message read by recipient or listener hears the message
- Message decoded – recipient works out what message means
- Message understood

At this point a response may be generated, starting the cycle again as it is coded into a message. The message is sent by the sender, received by the recipient and decoded. The message is then understood and the cycle repeats, as shown overleaf.

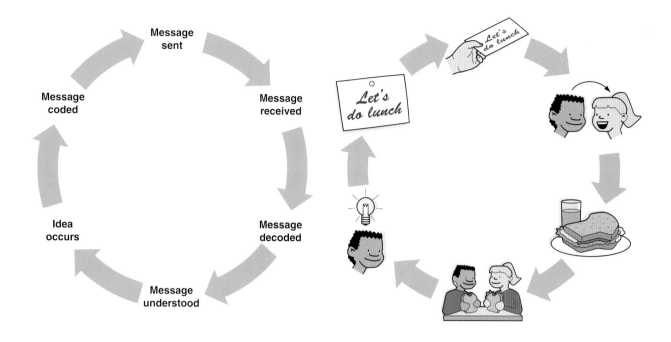

Activity 4

For P2.
Now draw your own example of a communication cycle.
What might go wrong with the cycle?

2 Understand factors that influence communication and interpersonal interactions in health and social care settings

The majority of this information relates to how well we get messages, ideas and feelings across to our service users. Therefore, when thinking about barriers to communication, you need to reflect on your own practice, something you will learn how to do in Unit 6 which is linked to your work experience.

Imagine situations you have been in whilst undertaking work experience or in class with your peers and tutors. This should help you to improve your practice and recognise any areas for improvement.

First, let's think about our service users and their needs. Not all service users are the same and certainly do not present with the same needs.

Two effective ways to assess service users' needs are:

● **Maslow's Hierarchy of Needs:**

● **PIES:**
  ● **P**hysical – need for food, water, warmth
  ● **I**ntellectual – need to develop concepts such as language, a sense of 'me', idea of colours, size, shapes
  ● **E**motional – the need to belong and to be loved, to be valued
  ● **S**ocial – the need for companionship

Maslow's Hierarchy of Needs

This is a theory put forward by Abraham Maslow (1908–1970), who suggested that the goal in human life is personal growth and to meet that goal, basic needs must first be met. The needs range from basic physical survival to higher-level needs.

To aid service users to meet their basic needs and to reach this goal, good communication with service users is essential.

Activity 5

Study Maslow's Hierarchy and suggest what needs may be assessed with your communication skills and how effective communication helps your service users. The following are some suggestions to help you.

Level 1: Basic physical needs should be met:
- Are you in pain?
- What sort of food do you like/dislike?
- Are you warm enough?

Level 2: This ensures that the patient is comfortable. Communication skills help to give a feeling of security.
- Do you require visitors, walking stick, contact buzzer?

Level 3: Effective communication skills enable service users to comfortably express their emotions and show affection to others. Take time with your service users.
- How do you feel today?
- Non-verbal communication – gestures, a hand on their shoulder – may be comforting.

Level 4: Positive communication allows service users to have self-esteem. It enables the service users to have a voice and feel valued and listened to. Listening skills are very valuable in the communication cycle.

Level 5: Positive communication will enable service users to grow and share ideas and will enable you to negotiate changes in their circumstances.

PIES

This is another way of classifying needs in health, social care and early years (see Activity 6).

Activity 6

Think of a service user at your work placement and assess their communication needs with the help of PIES. Then make suggestions as to how to resolve them. Follow the example below:

1. Physical – does the service user have a sensory impairment?
2. Intellectual/language – is English the service user's second language/does the service user use signs/symbols?
3. Emotional – is the service user able to express their feelings or thoughts? Does the service user require a counsellor?
4. Social – does the service user require an advocate to help them?

3 Know how patients/service users may be assisted by effective communication

It is increasingly common to meet service users in our care settings who may be unable to communicate effectively, so it is vital that we recognise this and assist them appropriately. Service users may have specific communication styles, for example:

- sign language
- use of pictures and symbols
- technology
- variations in accent, dialect or language

Activity 7

Stephen Hawking, born in 1942, is a famous scientist who was diagnosed with motor neurone disease at the age of 21. Limited mobility in all his limbs means that he is confined to a wheelchair, but although his voice was affected and he uses a voice synthesiser to communicate, he still writes books and scientific papers and delivers lectures at universities.
Visit his website – www.hawking.org.uk – and find out how he used to communicate before he used the synthesiser. Follow the disability link.

Consider the case studies below and with a partner think of ways you could help them to communicate. Some ideas have been suggested. This will help you with P4 in your assignment.

Case Study 1

You are caring for Mr Johnson who is 78 years old and is recovering from a stroke. His speech is slurred and difficult to understand. This is making him frustrated, anxious and occasionally short tempered.

Ideas:

- flash cards
- pen and paper
- simple hand gestures
- advocates

Case Study 2

In the GP surgery Ms Kubo has brought her son for his immunisations but is unsure about the programme on offer and speaks very little English as it is her second language.

Ideas:

- interpreter/translator
- advocate
- simple signs/symbols
- non-verbal communication

Case Study 3

In a school placement you are helping the class teacher support Molly, who has a hearing impairment and has had a cochlear implant. She has some hearing but not a full range of sounds.

Ideas:

- British Sign Language skills
- signs/symbols
- Makaton – www.makaton.org

Activity 8

This is helpful when looking at P4 for your assignment.
Think about your placement and some particular communication needs of your service users – they may be adults or children. Make a list of words and phrases that would help to convey messages. Put these into pictures and symbols/flashcards. You may want to devise a set of them as a class, with a theme such as:

1 food
2 personal hygiene
3 travel
4 feelings

There are many things which may hinder communication with our service users which could lead to misunderstanding, frustration or even aggression. The spider diagrams opposite illustrate a list of barriers which we may come across.

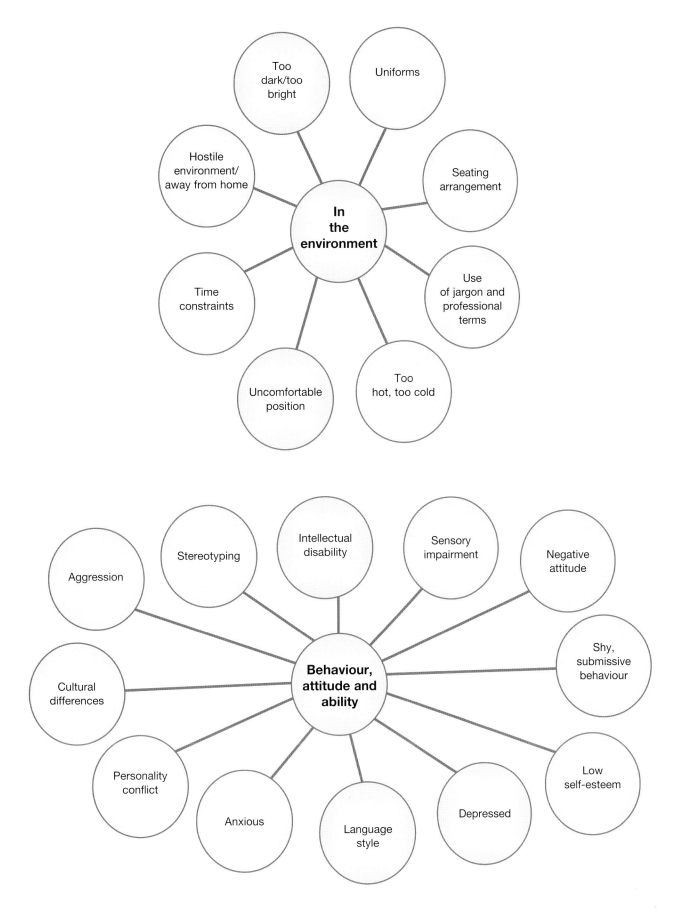

Activity 9

This will help with P3 for your assignment.
Devise a table with a list of some of the barriers we have identified,
then **describe** how care workers should help to overcome them.
You will find some suggestions below which will help with your descriptions:

BARRIER	HOW TO OVERCOME
Language differences	• Use translators or an interpreter • Use signs or symbols • Use short sentences • Increase your skills and learn a new language • Non-verbal communication – gestures and actions
Submissive behaviour	• Environment should be non-threatening • Don't use jargon • Use of advocate • Good listening skills • Allow time • Use of a counsellor

Support services available

The care value base (discussed in Unit 2) is essential when looking at how we support service users' communication. It is important as care workers to remember that just because service users have a different language, style or way of communicating does not mean that they cannot communicate.

We should always:

● empower the service user
● promote their rights
● maintain their confidentiality

If they are unable to communicate fully by themselves it is important that we support them in this or put them in touch with a service or tool which can. Technology can also be very useful to assist with communication requirements.

Activity 10

With the three care values in mind, devise a set of guidelines for care workers which uses their communication skills to enable service users to feel supported in the care setting. For example:

- Always ask the service user what they would prefer to be called
- Allow the service user a choice of menu
- Promote independent skills – dressing, eating, mobility
- Keep service user information in a secure place

Not only can we support our service users in the way we look after them but we can use the services available. Consider the list below and discuss what their role is and how we may use them. Find out whether you have these services at your care setting.

1 advocate
2 interpreter
3 translator
4 speech therapist
5 counsellor
6 psychologist

Activity 11

This will be useful when looking at M2 in your assignment.
Visit the following web links and prepare an information leaflet for service users who have sensory impairments. Make suggestions about the technology available to them for different aspects of their lives, e.g. work, travel, safety, cooking.

- www.rnib.org.uk – then follow the link to the shop
- www.rnid.org.uk – then follow the link to the shop

Include what technology can be used to assist service users with sensory impairments and how useful it will be for them.

Remember

You are not expected to have all the answers and you will be respected for being open, honest and truthful.

Support from your team

To ensure that the relationship between carer, service user and organisation runs smoothly, it is important to remember that if you are unable to answer service users' questions or provide a service which a service user requires, you should pass on the matter to another member of your health and social team who will be able to deal with the situation. Working as a team benefits service users and staff alike.

4 Be able to demonstrate own communication skills in a caring role

Communication skills are used with relatives, friends and health and social care workers too. If your tutor observes you communicating with a service user or other worker, you may be able to count this as witness testimony for your portfolio.

Activity 12

Towards P5.
Use a case study from your placement. Remember to keep confidentiality, so do not give the person's name. Explain how you have used *non-verbal* communication skills such as smiling to support a patient or service user.
- Where was it?
- Who was there?
- What happened?
- Why did you use this method?
- How effective was it? Did it work? How do you know?

Activity 13

Towards P5.
Give an example from your placement where you have used *verbal* communication with:
1 other workers
2 relatives or friends of service users
3 service users.

For each one answer these questions:
- Where was it?
- Who was there?
- What happened?
- Why did you use this method?
- How effective was it? Did it work? How do you know?
- What was the difference in your verbal communication between these interactions?

SUMMARY

After working through this unit you should be able to:

- explain effective communication

- explain interpersonal interaction

- explain factors that influence communication and interpersonal interactions

- give examples of this from health and social care settings

- explain how patients/service users may be assisted by effective communication

- demonstrate your own communication skills in a caring role.

Grading grid

In order to pass this unit, the evidence that the learner presents for assessment needs to demonstrate that they can meet all of the learning outcomes for the unit. The criteria for a pass grade describe the level of achievement required to pass this unit.

GRADING CRITERIA

TO ACHIEVE A PASS GRADE THE EVIDENCE MUST SHOW THAT THE LEARNER IS ABLE TO:	TO ACHIEVE A MERIT GRADE THE EVIDENCE MUST SHOW THAT, IN ADDITION TO THE PASS CRITERIA, THE LEARNER IS ABLE TO:	TO ACHIEVE A DISTINCTION GRADE THE EVIDENCE MUST SHOW THAT, IN ADDITION TO THE PASS AND MERIT CRITERIA, THE LEARNER IS ABLE TO:
P1 describe different types of communication and interpersonal interaction, using examples relevant to health and social care settings		
P2 describe the stages of the communication cycle	M1 explain how the communication cycle may be used to communicate difficult, complex and sensitive issues	
P3 describe factors that may influence communication and interpersonal interactions with particular reference to health and social care settings		
P4 identify how the communication needs of patients/service users may be assisted, including non-verbal communication	M2 explain the specific communication needs of patients/service users may have that require support, including the use of technology	D1 analyse how communication in health and social care settings assists patients/service users and other key people

GRADING CRITERIA

TO ACHIEVE A PASS GRADE THE EVIDENCE MUST SHOW THAT THE LEARNER IS ABLE TO:	TO ACHIEVE A MERIT GRADE THE EVIDENCE MUST SHOW THAT, IN ADDITION TO THE PASS CRITERIA, THE LEARNER IS ABLE TO:	TO ACHIEVE A DISTINCTION GRADE THE EVIDENCE MUST SHOW THAT, IN ADDITION TO THE PASS AND MERIT CRITERIA, THE LEARNER IS ABLE TO:
P5 describe two interactions that they have participated in, in the role of a carer, using communication skills to assist patients/service users		
P6 review the effectiveness of own communication skills in the two interactions undertaken.	M3 explain how own communication skills could have been used to make the interactions more effective.	D2 analyse the factors that influenced the interactions undertaken.

Equality, Diversity and Rights in Health and Social Care

This unit looks at how equality, diversity and upholding rights are fundamental in promoting effective delivery of health and social care services. It looks at discriminatory practice and its effects and how anti-discriminatory practice can be promoted.

Learning Outcomes

On completion of this unit you should be able to:

1 Understand the concepts of equality, diversity and rights in relation to health and social care
2 Understand discriminatory practice in health and social care
3 Understand how national initiatives promote anti-discriminatory practice in health and social care
4 Understand how anti-discriminatory practice is promoted in health and social care settings

1 Understand the concepts of equality, diversity and rights in relation to health and social care

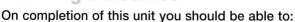

The benefits of diversity to society

We live in a diverse society. There are many benefits to a diverse society. As well as not respecting people, not respecting diversity is unfair and frequently illegal. Diversity can have benefits to society for everyone, from both a social and cultural perspective and an economic one.

Cultural enrichment
Different cultures have benefited from diversity

The arts
Many contemporary artists have origins in other cultures, e.g. Bob Marley

Food
Many foods available to us, such as curries, have origins in other cultures

Social and cultural benefits

Language
Many phrases that we use have origins in a variety of cultures, e.g. OK

Education
Benefits from diversity

Stephen Hawking and Trevor McDonald have made a contribution to today's society, yet represent some of the diversity that exists.

KEY CONCEPTS

Diversity means being different.

Activity 1

Pick one of the areas in the diagram above. Research the contribution made in this field by people from different backgrounds.

Stephen Hawking

Trevor McDonald

There are economic benefits to diversity such as employment expertise. A diverse society means we benefit from the contribution people can offer. This could be through the skills offered to the workforce. If this is not allowed or employment and education are subjected to a negative experience, the benefits offered by people will be lost.

Tolerance

Tolerance is important to ensure that everyone has equal opportunities. It is recognition of the fact that everyone is different. This can lead to *social cohesion*, which means that groups within society will reflect unity.

Respecting diversity means accepting and appreciating that all service users are different. This leads to promoting fair and equal opportunities.

Terminology

There are many key terms used to describe and express concepts of equality and diversity within health and social care. It is necessary to understand these concepts to be able to discuss the importance of equality and diversity and the issues surrounding these.

- *Equality*: This is about ensuring that people have equal access to health and social care.
- *Equity*: This is a principle that all people should have equal opportunities. This is not about everyone having the same wealth or power but about ensuring that everyone has the same rights in law. It also means that individuals should not be discriminated against. It is based on the moral right of all individuals to equal opportunities.
- *Diversity*: This is about accepting that everybody is different. People can bring many varied things into society and as such society is diverse. We have the right to be different with views and opinions and these must be respected. It is not just about being politically correct or being a good society, it is about creating social cohesion and harmony through challenging and changing people's attitudes towards different cultures.
- *Rights*: These are important within care, otherwise you are not giving appropriate care. By not accepting that people have the same rights as you, you are denying them their human rights.
- *Opportunity*: If equality and diversity are ensured, everyone should have an equal chance to achieve their potential in society.
- *Difference*: This is the quality that makes someone unlike someone else.
- *Overt discrimination*: This is one of two forms of discrimination. It is when you knowingly treat someone unfairly on the basis of, for example, race or gender.
- *Covert discrimination*: This type of discrimination tends to be more subtle. Although it may be unintentional, it still has severe consequences.
- *Stereotyping*: This is based on prejudice and means holding beliefs that all members of a group are the same. This information is often based on negative beliefs and is inaccurate. The person is not seen as an individual.
- *Labelling*: By labelling someone you are applying a stereotype to them. People may sometimes live up to this labelling and discrimination often results. It is

Activity 2

Where do our prejudices come from? How do we form our ideas of groups of people? How could you challenge your prejudices?

used to 'put people down'. Individuals or groups who fall within a negative stereotype start from an inferior position and thus lack power and influence.

- *Prejudice*: This means having a pre-conceived idea about somebody or a group of people. It can take many different forms, is often deep seated and can be powerful. It is based on fear or lack of knowledge and can be a reflection of power.
- *Disadvantage*: This is something that will count against someone and put somebody in a weaker situation than someone else.
- *Beliefs and values*: These are things that are your attitude or way of life. They are what are important to a person. These generally come from someone's upbringing or their experiences. It is important to remember not to treat someone differently on the basis of their views.
- *Vulnerability*: This is something that makes someone open to emotional or physical danger or harm.
- *Abuse*: This is the neglect or mistreatment of individuals, generally those who are vulnerable, and can be sexual, physical, emotional or financial.
- *Empowerment*: One of the fundamental principles of care work, empowerment is about enabling people to take control over their lives through choices and be as independent as possible.
- *Independence*: This means that someone has the freedom not to be dependent or controlled by someone else, an organisation or the state.
- *Interdependence*: This is when people are dependent on each other. This may be through mutual assistance or cooperation.

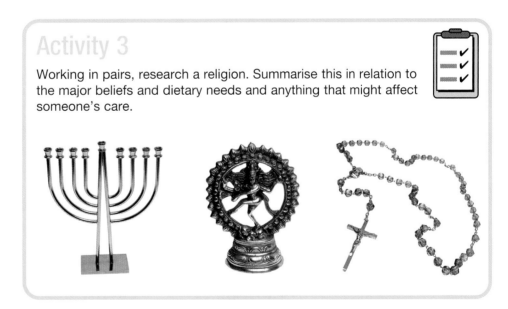

Activity 3

Working in pairs, research a religion. Summarise this in relation to the major beliefs and dietary needs and anything that might affect someone's care.

Discrimination against specific groups has its own terminology. This includes racism, sexism (on the basis of gender) and homophobia (on the basis of sexuality).

Understanding discriminatory practice in health and social care

There are many health and social care settings. Some examples are shown in the diagram below. Each of these settings will have its own policies and procedures to promote equality and diversity.

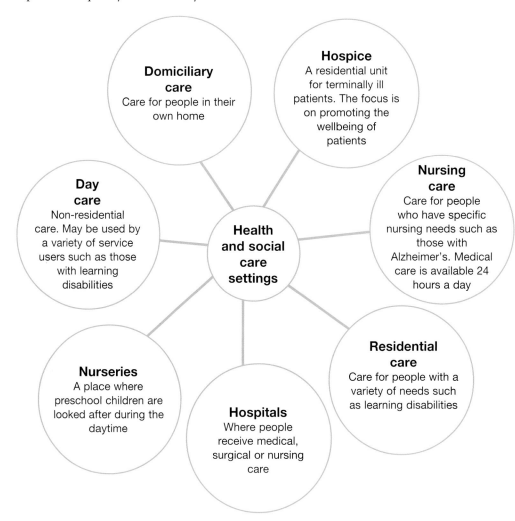

Active promotion of equality and individual rights

Within each of these care settings there should be an 'active promotion of equality and individual rights'. This means actually doing something to ensure that equality and rights exist within the workplace.

There are a number of ways that this can be addressed, including putting legislation, policies and procedures into practice. These policies and procedures reflect legislation that promotes equality.

One of the main ways that equality and individual rights can be promoted is through the care value base.

The care value base

There are three main care values.

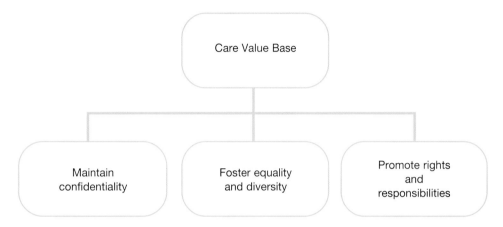

- *Maintain confidentiality*. This means not divulging information to anyone who does not have the right to that information. There are a few exceptions when you can break confidentiality. These are when the person is at risk to themselves or to others, or if they are at risk from abuse. Confidentiality can be maintained in a number of ways, such as not talking to or about service users in a public place, making sure records are marked 'confidential' and read only by those who should read them, or ensuring that computer records have passwords. Confidentiality is important as it builds trust between service users and staff members and can protect them. The principles of confidentiality should be reflected in policies, procedures and guidelines.
- *Foster equality and diversity*. This is all about understanding the implications of prejudice, stereotyping and labelling and the effects that these have on service users. It is important to appreciate your own beliefs and assumptions about diversity and acknowledge how these may impact upon practice. It is also important to recognise the benefits that diversity has on society. It ensures that everyone is treated as an individual.
- *Promote rights and responsibilities*. People have many rights within health and social care. These include the right to be different, to have choice and dignity within health and social care and to be safe and secure. Care workers have the responsibility to adhere to these rights, but also have their own rights. These include working in a safe environment and not being subjected to abuse.

Activity 4

Which of these care values are not being observed in the following case study? What should be carried out instead and what would you do to challenge the situation if you were the manager?

Case Study

Sheila works in a care home for older people with dementia. She sees Carla, another assistant, dress Mr Phillips. Carla chooses the clothes that he should wear without consulting Mr Phillips.

After he is dressed Mr Phillips comes down for his breakfast. He is a strict orthodox Jew. The new care assistant Tim is giving Mr Phillips his breakfast and has not been told about any dietary needs that Mr Phillips has. Mr Phillips requests a visit to the synagogue and this is denied.

Carla, Tim and Sheila then write up the notes from the shift. Sheila finishes her section and leaves Carla and Tim to finish their section. Carla and Tim forget to put their notes away and are still talking about the shift and the demands of Mr Phillips when they go for a drink after work.

Activity 5

Think back to your placement. Where have you applied the care values in your work placement? Compare your examples with someone else's examples.

KEY CONCEPTS

Putting the patient/service user at the heart of service provision – to give someone control and power over their lives, such as making decisions which means that they are as independent as possible.

It is always important that the service user is central to any provision that exists. This can be by providing active support so that you do things with the service user rather than for them. Actively involving the service user can lead to empowerment. Centres can ensure the participation of service users within provision, such as involving them in the running of the centre and helping to organise trips, and promoting individuals' rights, such as giving a choice of food at meal times.

Sometimes there may be tensions between rights and responsibilities and this may mean that a service user's rights may be compromised.

Activity 6

Read the following case study and decide where the tensions are and what you would do in the situation. Compare your views with someone else's.

Case Study

Tim works in a residential home for people with learning disabilities. A service user, David, has suddenly decided he wants to go to the shops. However, if David goes out, it will mean leaving the other service users with one member of staff.

Now make up your own case study illustrating some of the tensions between rights and responsibilities. What would you do in the situation?

Anti-discriminatory practice

This is when you act against any kind of discrimination, whatever the basis. Examples of anti-discriminatory practice include providing access to any necessary aids, having staff or service user representatives for meetings, making laws, charters, policies and procedures available to all, putting the patient/service user at the heart of service provision.

Staff development and training

This is crucial to promote equality through the service. This may also include teaching service users about confidentiality and that they have the right to see their own files. It may be necessary to understand the methods of communication available or use interpreters. Training has to be revisited and refreshed to ensure that everyone is up to date with developments. Sometimes workplaces will have a mentor system to ensure that training is carried out in practice. A mentor can also be a point of contact for new staff. Employers should ensure that they use fair and ethical methods of interviewing and hiring staff and that equal opportunities are monitored and reviewed as necessary.

Induction of new staff should cover the practical implications of confidentiality, such as how to record, report, store and share information. Staff should understand their role in relation to the policies and procedures of each workplace.

Activity 7

Go to your work placement and ask about their induction process. Look at the sections on confidentiality and rights and note any key points that you should check within your placement. Check with your supervisor if you are unsure of anything.

Individual rights

All service users have a number of rights that should be respected within health and social care settings. Even though they are receiving health and social care services, they are humans and deserve to be treated as such. Rights are often protected by legislation.

Some of these rights include those in the table on the next page.

Activity 8

Read the following case study and decide which rights are or are not being respected.

Faye works at Rose Cottage Care Home. This is her day.

Case Study

Faye arrives at work at 7am. She is a little hungover. Before she starts her cleaning tasks, she has a lie down on the sofa until her shift partner, Tim, arrives.

Faye and Tim begin getting up the residents. One resident, Mark, requests a lie in. Faye replies, 'No, you can have a lie in on Sunday, you must get up now – it's your turn.'

While Tim and Faye are bathing residents they leave the doors open so they can chat about the night before. When Tim goes to dress Jude, Jude wants to wear her blue jumper which is downstairs, having been washed by the night staff. Tim cannot be bothered to go down to get it and tells Jude it is still in the wash and she should wear her red one. Jude wants to wear something else but Tim does not (or pretends not to) hear her, as he continues to chat to Faye about her night out.

Another resident uses British Sign Language, but unfortunately neither Tim nor Faye is trained to communicate in this way. They therefore have to guess at what the resident is trying to say.

Mavis is up and dressed by this stage. Mavis is Faye's favourite resident and often Faye will give her extra support and activities.

Tim and Faye want to take out some of the residents. Ignoring the risk assessment, they take out more residents than they should and leave some with John, a new member of staff.

It is nearly lunchtime and Tim and Faye make everyone beans on toast. After lunch Tim and Faye write up the notes from the shift in the office. They do not discuss this with the residents and as it is shift changeover, they leave the notes on the side.

RIGHT	HOW THIS RIGHT CAN BE DEMONSTRATED
To be respected. To be treated as an individual.	Through communication and how service users are treated. Showing interest in service users and valuing them as people. Ensuring that dignity and privacy are maintained.
To be treated equally and not discriminated against. People are not the same and should not be treated as the same, but should be given equal access to services.	By ensuring that all service users have equal access to services. Can also be demonstrated by involving people in decisions attempting a redistribution of power.
To be treated in a dignified way.	If this is not ensured, individuals may feel they are not worth anything. You should treat individuals how they would expect to be treated. This can promote self-esteem and reduce any threat the person may feel.
To be allowed privacy. This can involve having a space which can be entered only by consent. This saves the person being either humiliated or embarrassed.	People may need assistance with personal hygiene. It is important to remember that this is more than just carrying out a simple task. Privacy can be maintained by simple efforts such as ensuring that a door is closed when carrying out personal hygiene tasks.
To be treated as an individual.	Showing interest in a person, their views and their preferences.
To be protected from danger and harm. A service user should be safe and secure in their environment. This is particularly important if you are working with vulnerable people.	Carry out a risk assessment. This can relate to individuals' possessions and their relationships with other people. It is important to maintain this so that an individual does not feel violated. This can be carried out by checking identities and providing a safe and secure place to store service users' valuable items.
To be allowed access to information about themselves.	Through being involved within meetings or discussing notes with service users before writing them up. If the service user cannot participate themselves, an advocate could be used.
To be able to communicate using their preferred methods of communication and language. Many of an individual's rights are dependent on being able to communicate them.	Ensuring that service users who require appropriate communication methods such as communication passports or sign language are accommodated within the setting. Active listening is more than just giving and receiving information. Poor communication can result in a lack of self-esteem. A carer can also check that what they said was correct and be clear in communication with people.
To be cared for in a way that meets their needs. There must be a focus on the needs of the person they are caring for.	Have services that put the service user at the centre of the process and ensure all needs (physical, emotional, social, intellectual, cultural) are taken into account.
To take account of service user choice. The service user must be at the centre of any planning (person-centred planning). Choice must be based on what people need and wish for.	To give service users as many options as possible. This could include what time to get up or go to bed or about treatment they receive. To be as independent as possible – if service users are to be deliberately restricted there should be clear reasons for doing this. If a person feels their choices are not being respected, their self-esteem will diminish. It is important that choices are realistic. A choice offered can be major or minor. Information offered should be maximised and choices should be offered where previously they did not exist.

Rights within health and social care settings

2 Understand discriminatory practice in health and social care

Although there are groups that may get discriminated against, it is important to remember that not everyone in that group may be subject to discrimination. Such groups include those from particular cultures, those with disabilities, and those who are discriminated against on the basis of age, social class, gender, sexuality, health status, family status or cognitive ability.

Cultures

People have a wide background which makes up their culture. This may include a person's ethnicity, social class, religion, sexuality or even where they live. Discrimination may occur when a judgement is made on the basis of a stereotype or prejudice.

Ethnicity

This involves being discriminated against on the basis of colour of skin or culture. This may be identified in different situations. For example, there is a general concentration of ethnic minorities in lower-paid occupations and they are underrepresented in senior positions. According to statistics from Social Trends, which shows trends in British society gathered from government information, in 1994 unemployment was highest among non-white groups.

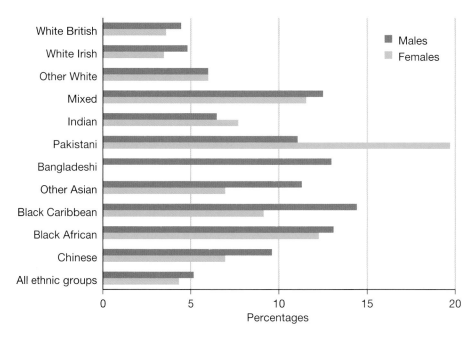

Unemployment rates, 1994
Source: National Statistics website – www.statistics.gov.uk

Age

According to the Office of National Statistics, a third of the labour force will be over 50 by 2020 (source: DTI, 2006). There is concern that older workers may face discrimination in areas of society, especially in employment and training. There is no evidence to suggest that a 20 year old will stay on longer at a company than a 40 year old. The government has recently introduced legislation, such as the Age Discrimination Laws in 2006, to prevent discrimination against older workers.

Sexuality

According to Stonewall, a campaign group that works for equality and justice for lesbians, gay men and bisexuals, the government's figures show that 5–7 per cent of the population are lesbian, gay or bisexual (source: www.stonewall.org). In the past, lesbian, gay and bisexual people have not had equal access within society. This can lead to both discrimination and people not being open about their sexuality for fear of discrimination.

Gender

There have been major changes and shifts in beliefs since equal rights were introduced in 1928. Women and men are not generally seen as having the same opportunities. Legislation such as the Equal Pay Act and the Sex Discrimination Act of 1975 have reduced this inequality. In spite of this legislation, there is still discrepancy in areas such as in pay.

In 2005, average hourly earnings for women working full-time were £11.67 and for men were £14.08. This gave a full-time gender pay gap of 17.1 per cent. Part-time women workers earned £8.68 on average – comparing this figure with men's average full-time earnings of £14.08 gives a part-time gender pay gap of 38.4 per cent (source: Social Trends).

Disability

Disability may be the result of physical, mental or sensory impairment. Disabled people may experience discrimination on the basis that they are not seen as 'normal', a product of the way in which disability is viewed. There are two ways of looking at disability – the medical and the social model. The medical model sees disability as the person themselves responsible for changing. The social model sees disability as society's responsibility to change.

In 2005 both disabled women and men had lower employment rates and higher unemployment rates than women and men who were not disabled (source: Equal Opportunities Commission). The difference in employment rates is largest for men: 52 per cent of disabled men work compared with 85 per cent of men who are not disabled, while 49 per cent of disabled women work compared with 75 per cent of women who are not disabled. Therefore disability has a severe impact on some chances within society.

Health status

A person's health status may cause them to be subject to discriminatory practice. This could include people who are HIV positive who may be seen as a risk to others. People with mental health conditions may also experience discrimination and prejudice. This is often based on people not understanding the causes and conditions, or story lines in television programmes such as soap operas being taken out of context.

Discriminatory practice

Discriminatory practice can occur on three levels. These three levels are not exclusive and can be the cause or effect of each other.

1   On an *individual* basis from the prejudice of others. This may include exclusion, insults or violence. An individual may be singled out and treated differently.
2   On an *institutional* level through the organisation failing to provide services. This can be the result of an organisation's rules, regulations and practices.
3   On a *structural* level, where whole communities and societies have discriminatory views or beliefs about certain people. A whole community can pass on discrimination. People see the world from their culture and this is a reflection on society.

Case Study: Stephen Lawrence

In 1993 Stephen Lawrence, a black British 18 year old, was murdered while waiting at a bus stop. His attackers are said to have shouted racist insults. However, the Crown Prosecution Service dropped the case due to insufficient evidence. Stephen's family brought a private prosecution, which acquitted the suspects of any charges.

The case received a wealth of media publicity. The then Home Secretary, Jack Straw, ordered a public inquiry which found cases of institutional racism in the way the investigation was carried out. The report, known as the Stephen Lawrence Inquiry or the Macpherson Report, made 70 recommendations to demonstrate zero tolerance of racism. Although this includes the police, it also wants improvements among other public bodies.

This case reflected discriminatory practice – on an individual level, Stephen Lawrence was singled out and murdered; on an institutional level, police handling of the case was seen as an example of institutional racism.

The way in which discriminatory practice is displayed can be either overt or covert. It can be overt through direct discrimination, such as 'Women need not apply'. It is obvious discriminatory practice which may be demonstrated through language or denying people their rights. Covert discrimination is harder to prove and is sometimes known as indirect discrimination. It is a more subtle way of discriminating against someone.

Activity 9

Which of the following is covert discrimination and which is overt discrimination?

● People over 50 need not apply.
● Applications now being taken for predominantly female course.

Discrimination can present itself in various ways. It may be through physical assault, verbal abuse, excluding people from activities or opportunities, avoiding people because they are different, sending out messages through negative, non-verbal communication or making assumptions that everyone should be treated the same. This results in devaluing people.

Discriminatory practice can occur through not upholding people's rights, such as being treated as an individual or cared for in a way that meets their needs. Consequently, labelling and stereotyping may result.

Effects

A person or group of people can be *marginalised* as a result of discrimination. Usually they are a minority group and as a consequence may be isolated from cultural, social and economic activities.

In the extreme, oppression can lead to abuse, murder or even genocide. On an individual basis it may create low self-esteem, poor self-image, negative self-worth or lowering of self-confidence. This can have a lasting effect on education achievements and progress at work, thus leading to a loss of motivation to achieve.

Disempowerment can cause people to become withdrawn and this in turn can lead to learned helplessness. The problem can be triggered by someone feeling they do not have control over decisions that are important in their lives. Stress itself has a number of consequences, such as tiredness. People can develop low self-worth, which can lead to mental illness such as depression. People then expect to be rejected or excluded. This can impact upon the whole person. They may not feel safe due to a threat of physical violence or verbal abuse. They may spend their life struggling with low self-esteem and unmet needs.

Discriminatory practice may also result in restricted opportunities. This can be in an economic way such as the unemployment of specific groups or ethnic minorities. In a broader societal way, prejudiced assumptions may become more popular, which can exacerbate the discriminatory cycle.

KEY CONCEPTS

Disempowerment is when people are deprived of choice; they are not consulted.

Activity 10

Relate the effects of discriminatory practice to Maslow's Hierarchy of Needs (see page 5).

Case Study

Tim lives at home with his long-term partner, David. Tim has difficulties in walking. He should be receiving physiotherapy from his community physiotherapist. His care plan states this should take place once a week. Tim's physiotherapist attends infrequently and does not telephone to inform Tim. Another of the physiotherapist's clients, Mr Taylor, has different experiences. Mr Taylor is married. The physiotherapist attends his appointments regularly and often pops by to check on progress and to see how his client is progressing.

What impact might the physiotherapist have on Tim's health and well-being?

How might it affect his physical, intellectual, emotional and social well-being?

3 Understand how national initiatives promote anti-discriminatory practice in health and social care

Conventions, legislation and regulations

There are many laws (legislation), conventions and regulations which govern our lives as citizens. It is not easy to keep up to date with all of them, especially when there are frequent changes to existing laws and many more new laws being created. There are some laws which apply only to England and Wales and some which apply only to Scotland. In addition to these laws there are conventions, which are also a type of law.

The Council of Europe was set up in 1950 to unite Europe. It is not the same as the European Union. The Council of Europe set up the Convention for the Protection of Human Rights and Fundamental Freedoms, also known as the **European Convention on Human Rights**, in 1950. The rights are set out in articles which ban torture and discrimination. Some of the articles give rights, for example Article 2 gives the right to life and Article 5 gives the right to liberty and security. You can find out more about the Council of Europe and the Court of Human Rights in Strasbourg by looking on the following websites: http://conventions.coe.int and www.echr.coe.int/ECHR.

In addition to European conventions, there are United Nations (UN) conventions. In 1989, the UN adopted the **Convention on the Rights of the Child**, which brought together international human rights for children.

Did you know?

In 1964:

● people letting rooms in London displayed signs saying: 'No Blacks, No Irish, No Dogs.'

● women doing the same job as men were not paid the same wage.

● women were discriminated against for jobs just because they were female.

See www.yourrights.org.uk

The guiding principles of the Convention on the Rights of the Child include the following:

- survival and development rights, which include rights to food, shelter, clean water, formal education and primary health care. There are specific sections covering the needs of child refugees, children with disabilities and children of minority groups.
- protection rights, which include protection from child abuse, neglect, exploitation and cruelty.
- participation rights, which entitle children to express opinions and to have a say in matters affecting their social, economic, religious, cultural and political life.

Member countries of the UN have to abide by this convention too. If you find this confusing, think of a family.

The parents may have some rules, such as the children have to be in bed by 9pm. One of the older children joins a karate club and the class does not finish until 10pm. There has to be a compromise. If you join a club, you have to abide by those rules as well as the rules you already live by. The UN and the European Court are like clubs, and they have their rules which Britain must accept if it wants to be in that club. Sometimes the rules do not agree. Sometimes the conventions and laws do not agree. Just like a family has to compromise on rules, the British government had to change the law to meet the requirements of the European Convention on Human Rights.

People have brought cases against the British government to the European Court of Human Rights since 1966. As a result some of the laws in Britain have had to change. In 1998, the Human Rights Act became law in Britain and was intended to give greater effect to the European Convention on Human Rights.

The European Convention on Human Rights gave people the means to fight discrimination. As a result, the British Parliament passed laws banning discrimination on the grounds of sex and race. Later legislation covered disability.

The Equal Pay Act 1970 established that men and women should get the same pay for the same job.

The Sex Discrimination Act 1975 was passed to protect men, women and transgendered people from discrimination on the grounds of gender. This act made it illegal to refuse a job or training to someone because of their gender.

The Equal Opportunities Commission (EOC) was established in order to make sure these laws were implemented.

You can find out more on the following websites:

- www.eoc.org.uk – the Equal Opportunities Commission
- www.womenandequalityunit.gov.uk/legislation – the government website for women and equality

On 1 October 2005 the Employment Equality (Sex Discrimination) Regulations 2005 came into force. This amended the 1970 Equal Pay Act and the 1975 Sex Discrimination Act to meet the requirements of European laws or directives about equal treatment for men and women with regard to access to employment, vocational training, promotion and working conditions.

The Children Act 1989:

- reformed the law relating to children, bringing together what had previously been complex and diverse laws
- made provision for local authority services for children in need and others
- amended the law with respect to children's homes, community homes, voluntary homes and voluntary organisations
- made provision with respect to fostering, childminding and day care for young children, and adoption

The Children Act 2004 looks at improving children's lives. The aim is to encourage joint planning, commissioning and delivery of services. This should reduce duplication, improve multi-disciplinary working, and increase accountability. Previously a child could be admitted to hospital with bruising and broken bones, yet no one contacted a social worker or reported suspected abuse. A child might be on the at-risk register, yet health care professionals were not told. This situation should no longer arise as services are encouraged to work together.

The legislation is enabling rather than prescriptive, which means different local authorities will interpret it differently, but there is a new duty on local authorities to promote the educational achievement of looked-after children.

The wider reform programmes are outlined in *Every Child Matters: Change for Children*.

Activity 11

Linking to P4, M1, D1.
- Find out more about *Every Child Matters* at www.everychildmatters.gov.uk and outline the key features of this policy.
- How might *Every Child Matters* influence anti-discriminatory practice in your local area?
- Evaluate the influence of *Every Child Matters* on organisational and personal practice in relation to anti-discriminatory practice.

Mental Health Act 1983

The Mental Health Act 1983 makes provision for the compulsory detention and treatment in hospital of those with mental disorders. A person may be admitted to hospital under Part 2 of the Act if there is a formal application by either an

Approved Social Worker (ASW) or the nearest relative, as described in the Act. The application must be supported by recommendations made by two qualified medical practitioners, one of whom must be approved for the purpose under the Act. Patients may apply to a tribunal to be considered for discharge.

The Mental Health (Northern Ireland) Order 1986 makes similar provision in Northern Ireland. This Act was amended in 2004 to clarify some issues.

The Mental Capacity Act 2005 provides a statutory framework to empower and protect vulnerable people who are not able to make their own decisions. It makes it clear who can take decisions, in which situations, and how they should go about this. It enables people to plan ahead for a time when they may lose capacity.

At the time of writing (spring 2007), both the Mental Health Act 1983 and the Mental Capacity Act 2005 are about to be amended and will include the Bournewood safeguards to 'protect the human rights of people with a mental disorder who lack capacity to consent to arrangements for their care, who are deprived of liberty in their own best interests but who are not detained under the Mental Health Act 1983'. *Source*: www.dh.gov.uk.

Race Relations Act 1976, Race Relations (Amendment) Act 2000

The 1976 legislation made racial discrimination illegal. The 2000 amendment requires public bodies to promote race equality. Schools, local authorities, hospitals must all abolish unlawful racial discrimination and promote equality of opportunity and good relations between people of different racial groups.

The Commission for Racial Equality (CRE) was set up to enforce the Race Relations Act. This means that anyone not following the requirements of the Act may be taken to court by the CRE. The Commission also produces guidelines and advice in the form of a Statutory Code of Practice to help employers, schools and other public bodies comply with the legislation.

Disability Discrimination Act 1995, Disability Discrimination Act 2005

For the first time, legislation was passed covering the needs of people with disabilities. Previously it was legal to refuse a job to someone because they had a disability. After the 1995 Act, it became illegal to do so. The Act gave people with disabilities rights in employment, education, access to goods and facilities and when buying land or property. For the first time, minimum standards were set requiring public transport to meet the needs of those with disabilities, although it was still difficult to travel by public transport if you used a wheelchair or were visually impaired.

The 1995 Act was amended in 2005 by a new Disability Discrimination Act which extended the powers of the 1995 Act. It became illegal for operators of public transport to discriminate against people with disabilities. This means that the rail service has to provide facilities so that disabled people can travel. This might mean ramps at stations, or help from a guard. Buses now have lower platforms to enable people with disabilities to board. Other changes included making it illegal for private clubs with 25 or more members to exclude disabled people and making it easier for disabled people to rent property. For the first time the definition of disability was extended to cover 'hidden' disabilities such as HIV, cancer and multiple sclerosis from the moment they are diagnosed. The Disability Rights Commission (DRC) was set up in December 2006 to enforce this legislation. See www.drc.org.uk.

Data Protection Act 1998

The Data Protection Act 1998 came into force on 1 March 2000, replacing the 1984 Data Protection Act (see www.ico.gov.uk). The Act applies to 'personal data', which is data about identifiable living individuals, and covers both personal data held electronically and manual or paper data held in structured files or easily accessible systems.

The Data Protection Act gives rights to individuals about whom information is held. It also requires those who record and use 'personal information' to follow the eight principles of good information handling. The eight principles require that data must be:

- fairly and lawfully processed
- processed for limited purposes
- adequate, relevant and not excessive
- accurate
- not kept for longer than is necessary
- processed in line with the data subject's rights
- secure
- not transferred to countries without adequate protection

Processing may be carried out only where one of the following conditions has been met:

- the individual has given his or her consent to the processing
- the processing is necessary for the performance of a contract with the individual
- the processing is required under a legal obligation
- the processing is necessary to protect the vital interests of the individual
- the processing is necessary to carry out public functions
- the processing is necessary in order to pursue the legitimate interests of the data controller or third parties (unless it could prejudice the interests of the individual).

Further provisions relating to the processing of sensitive data include data on racial or ethnic origin, political opinions, religious or other beliefs, trade union membership, health, sex life, criminal proceedings or other convictions. The Data Protection Act 1998 gives individuals the right of access to information held about them but forbids releasing that information to anyone else without permission, unless there is a legal requirement to do so.

The Freedom of Information Act 2000 (FOI Act) gives individuals the right to obtain access to official information consistent with the public interest and the need to protect confidential information. Many journalists use this to uncover information which might not otherwise be brought to public notice.

Two of the main features of the FOI Act are:

- a general right of access to information subject to certain conditions and exemptions
- a duty on a public body to inform any person who requests information

whether they hold the information and to communicate that information to the applicant unless one or more exemptions apply

Requests must be responded to within 20 working days of receipt of the request. Sometimes information cannot be released because it falls under the Data Protection Act.

Care Standards Act 2000, Nursing and Residential Care Homes Regulations 1984 (amended 2002)

The Care Standards Act 2000 replaces previous legislation such as the Registered Homes Act 1984 and amendments. The Act established a new Commission for Social Care Inspection (CSCI) with powers to register, regulate and inspect:

- domiciliary social care providers
- independent fostering agencies
- residential family centres
- boarding schools
- residential care homes for adults
- nursing homes
- children's homes

The 2000 Act was prescriptive, stating what must be done. This was in contrast to the 1984 legislation which allowed flexibility of interpretation. The 2000 Act set out legally required national minimum standards. Some of these standards, such as minimum room size, were difficult for small homes to meet and thus many of them closed. Under the CSCI, inspectors are powerful. They can demand to see documents about the running of a home and talk to service users in private about the care they receive. Many homes closed rather than meet the new stringent requirements. Despite these powers, however, there have been few prosecutions.

You can find out about the work of the CSCI and read inspections reports at www.csci.org.uk.

Activity 12

Linking to P4, M1, D1.
Using the CSCI website – www.csci.org.uk – find an inspection report for a home near you. Look at the checklist of statutory requirements towards the end of the report.

- What, if any, are issues for equality? Do wheelchair users have access to all public areas? Are people given a choice of food? Are they encouraged to be independent?
- How effective do you think the CSCI inspector's report is? Are there any unmet requirements from the last inspection? Look at how many times recommendations are made before being carried out.

The Employment Equality (Age) Regulations 2006

Did you know?

Legislation changes rapidly. The best way to keep up is to use the government website: www.direct.gov.uk

Since 1 October 2006, there is legal protection against age discrimination. The new laws apply to all employers, private and public sector, vocational training providers, trade unions, professional organisations, employer organisations and trustees and managers of occupational pension schemes. They cover employees of any age, and other workers, office holders, partners of firms and others. They cover recruitment, terms and conditions, promotions, transfers, dismissals and training. They do not cover provision of goods and services. The new laws make it illegal to discriminate for jobs and training on the grounds of age.

Codes of practice and charters

Did you know?

More changes are on the way! In 2007, the Commission for Equality and Human Rights (CEHR) enforces the Race Equality duty, the Disability Equality duty and the Gender duty. See more on www.cehr.org.uk.

Codes and charters are guidelines recommending what should happen. Unlike the laws, conventions and regulations already mentioned, they are not legally binding.

Social workers are encouraged to register with the General Social Care Council (GSCC). The Council produces codes of practice for social care workers and employers.

In Wales the Care Council for Wales fills a similar function and in Northern Ireland it is the Northern Ireland Social Care Council.

Activity 13

Linking to P5.
Work in threes and check out the codes of conduct on each website. What differences, if any, can you find?

- www.gscc.org.uk
- www.ccwales.org.uk
- www.niscc.info

Nurses, midwives and specialist community public health nurses have to abide by the NMC code of professional conduct: standards for conduct, performance and ethics published by the Nursing and Midwifery Council.

The code states that as a registered nurse, midwife or specialist community public health nurse, you must:

- respect the patient or service user as an individual
- obtain consent before you give any treatment or care
- cooperate with others in the team
- protect confidential information
- maintain your professional knowledge and competence

● be trustworthy
● act to identify and minimise the risk to patients and service users

Source: www.nmc-uk.org

Activity 14

Linking to P4 and P5.
Compare the codes of conduct from the General Social Care Council and the Nursing and Midwifery Council. List the similarities and list the differences in relation to anti-discriminatory practice.

Charters and entitlement to services

Patient Advice and Liaison Services (PALS)

The 1991 Patient's Charter was abolished in 1997 and replaced by PALS, which is intended to involve the public and patients in the NHS. It does not set out rights but rather provides:

● confidential advice and support to patients, families and their carers
● information on the NHS and health-related matters
● confidential assistance in resolving problems and concerns quickly
● information on and explanations of NHS complaints procedures and how to get in touch with someone who can help. More information can be found from the Complaints policy section of the Department of Health website (see link below)
● information on how you can get more involved in your own health care and the NHS locally (see link 'Make Time for Health')
● a focal point for feedback from patients to inform service developments
● an early warning system for NHS trusts, primary care trusts and patient and public involvement forums by monitoring trends and gaps in services and reporting these to the trust management for action

Source: www.dh.gov.uk

The focus is on involvement rather than entitlement to services. Patient and Public Involvement (PPI) forums actively seek volunteers to represent the views of the public in health matters. See the Commission for Patient and Public Involvement in Health website: www.cppih.org.

Activity 15

Linking to P4, M1, D1.
Produce a leaflet about PPI forums. The leaflet should be suitable to explain the role of PPI forums to the ordinary person.
What problems might you anticipate the forums will have in recruiting volunteers?

Organisational policies and procedures

Every organisation providing health and social care must have policies promoting the rights of service users.

Activity 16

Linking to P4.
At placement, ask for copies of any policies or procedures they have to cover service users' rights.

● Do they have a residents' committee?

● Do they have a complaints procedure?

● Is there an equal opportunities policy?

● Are service users and relatives able to voice concerns in confidence?

● How are service users' individual needs met under the sex discrimination, race relations and disability legislations?

Make a poster explaining what policies and procedures there are at your placement. Compare this with the poster of a student who is at a different placement. If you are not at a placement, use the CSCI website to get an inspection report and find the information from there.

In 'Making Choices: Taking Risks', a discussion paper published by the (CSCI), older people expressed their views about the quality of care they would like. They wanted support at the right time to help them deal with risks without losing their independence. The report found that poor quality care created risks for older people which they could not control. Just imagine what it would be like if you had to live with strangers, some of whom were suffering from dementia. How would you feel?

The report said that 'the key challenge for social care is to shift the balance towards supporting individuals who choose to take informed risks in order to improve the quality of their lives'. Older people want to remain independent even if they have to take risks to do so, but the report found that 'older people continue to experience age discrimination from care services and are not always afforded the dignity and respect they have a right to expect'.

Training of carers is important to ensure they have the right attitudes and skills to support people through change and to adapt to ageing. Frontline staff need to be better trained so that, rather than making decisions for people, they are encouraged and supported to help people make choices that will enhance their quality of life. Organisations and individuals with an interest in promoting the well-being of older people need to consider whether they have got the right balance between enabling the personal choices of individuals versus the perceived risk to organisations if things go wrong.

Would you like to live in a home where you are not allowed to practise your religion or make a cup of tea or even go to bed when you want? The CSCI asserts that it is important to balance health and safety risks against the need to maintain independence.

Activity 17

Linking to P4.
Explain how the discussion paper 'Making Choices: Taking Risks' can be used to promote anti-discriminatory practice in a care home. Think of discrimination which can occur around age, disability, sex and race.

Advocacy means support or encouragement. The following case study is an example of support in action.

Case Study: Sandwell People First

'I wanted to check to see if homes were up to standard,' explains Steven Ellis, who was one of four people with learning difficulties who were asked to help inspect 45 registered care homes in Birmingham and Solihull in 2005 and 2006.

They were all called 'Experts by Experience' because living their lives with a learning difficulty makes them experts in their own right and a valuable addition to the inspection team. Sandwell People First supported the Experts throughout the project.

Alison Ridge was one of the inspectors who worked with the Experts by Experience. She was impressed by their approach. 'The Experts looked at the services and asked, "Would I accept this in my life or for my friends?" It was very personal for them, which added a lot of value to the inspection. Also in many cases, when the Experts spoke to people living in the homes, they were able to find out information and were told things that I would never have been told.'

Copyright © 2007 Commission for Social Care Inspection (CSCI), www.csci.org.uk

Activity 18

Linking to P5 and M2.
What are the advantages of using advocates? What difficulties may arise when using advocates? Refer to the case study above if you have no experience of advocacy from your placement.

KEY CONCEPTS

Ethics is another word for moral values, beliefs and principles. Ethics help people to distinguish right from wrong.

4 Understand how anti-discriminatory practice is promoted in health and social care settings

Active promotion of anti-discriminatory practice

The Nursing and Midwifery Council sets standards for the conduct, performance and ethics of members. Care planning, a key role for nurses and social workers, is a way of putting the service user at the heart of service provision. Whatever the format of the care plan, the service user or patient should be involved with planning their care.

The following case study is an example of good practice. See whether you can work out why and then check with the comment at the end of the case study.

Case Study

Name of project: U-Turn
Based: East London
Work: Supporting women to leave street prostitution

Eighty-five per cent of street prostitutes are homeless or rough sleepers. They are the hidden homeless – those who do not sleep on the streets but on the floor of a friend's place; or are trapped in an abusive relationship with their pimp or boyfriend; or stay in a squat or disused buildings.

Because of their lifestyle, they do not come into contact with many of the other homelessness charities. They are not visible rough sleepers at night and they are seldom out and about during the day.

U-Turn meets them on the streets when they work – three nights a week in the London boroughs of Tower Hamlets and Newham. The outreach provides basic practical needs, such as food, hot drinks and condoms, as well as advice and information on available services.

'The women are instinctively mistrustful,' says director Rio Vella. 'Only by going out regularly and meeting the women on their territory on their terms have we been able to slowly build their trust. They find it difficult to cope with being sent from one agency to another, to get help with their health, their housing, their drug habit, and so on.'

U-Turn also runs a centre where women can freshen up. Vella says, 'Being homeless, many don't have access to washing facilities, and this adds to their low self-esteem, and reduces their willingness to engage with the very agencies that are trying to help them.'

'This is about treating the women with respect and dignity. No one has ever done that for them before. We aim to reinforce their self-worth, rebuild their self-confidence and support them to make their own positive choices in life.'

Source: first published on www.communitycare.co.uk

Comment

In this example, outreach care workers talk to the women and provide practical help. They do not insist the women give up prostitution, but instead give them information so that when the women feel able to change their lives, they will know how to get help.

Carl Rogers, a humanist psychologist, whom you will read about in Unit 8, developed the Person-Centred approach which applies to all interactions between people. This forms the basis of good-quality social and health care.

No one expects a patient or service user to be an expert, but they should be consulted and given a choice where possible, putting the patient/service user at the heart of service provision. This involves providing active support consistent with the beliefs, culture and preferences of the individual, supporting individuals in expressing their needs and preferences, empowering individuals, promoting individuals' rights, choices and wellbeing.

Sometimes individual rights have to be balanced with the rights of others, especially when accommodation is shared. Here is another case study from Community Care, this time where there is an imbalance of rights and there is conflict.

Activity 19

Linking to P5, M2.

Case Study: Get me out of this house!

The names have been changed.

Situation: Adam Silver is 27 years old and has Asperger's syndrome. He has been placed by social services into a shared house with two women. The house is staffed by workers from a voluntary organisation for two hours in the morning and two hours in the evening. The two women are recovering drug addicts, receiving additional support from the hospital outreach team. *Problem*: Adam has told his brother, Joe, that the women have lots of male visitors who pay them for sex and they use the money to buy drugs. They have told Adam not to tell anyone about this. Last month Adam went to see his brother and was very upset. He said that one of the men had said that Adam had to 'do sex' with him. Adam said the man was nasty and started to hit one of the women. Joe has been to the house and was concerned to find that most of Adam's clothes had disappeared, as had the TV/DVD player Joe and his wife gave him for Christmas. Adam has no idea where these items are. Joe has been in touch with social services, which pays for the placement. A worker there told Joe that Adam was an adult and could have sex with whom he liked and that it was likely that Adam had disposed of the TV and clothes. Adam is very unhappy and says that he wants to run away.

Source: first published on www.communitycare.co.uk

Activity 19 (continued)

1   Do you think running away will solve the problem? Explain your answer.
2   What could a care worker do to support Adam? Try to think of rights and responsibilities of:
    ● the other residents
    ● Adam
    ● the care worker
3   How could the care worker show anti-discriminatory practice?

You can find out how social workers would respond by checking the website www.communitycare.co.uk/Articles/2006/10/19/56126/Get+me+out+of+this+house.html

People with learning difficulties are sometimes denied their rights to choose who they live with just because they have learning difficulties. This is discrimination. Older people are sometimes denied choice just because they are old. This too is discrimination.

According to Age Concern, older people are sometimes discriminated against on the grounds of age. There is an upper age limit of 70 for breast cancer screening. Sometimes the term 'bed blockers' is applied to people who are ready to be discharged but cannot be sent home because of social circumstances. Often older people are in this situation and may be discriminated against by not being given choice between a care home, sheltered housing or help at home.

What can you do as a nurse or social worker? You can inform people of their rights and where they can get help and advice. The PALS service can provide advice. A patient may be entitled to a review before discharge. If social care is needed, there must be an assessment of the needs of the service user and their carer. Financial help may be available in the form of direct payments so that service users can purchase their own care.

It is the duty of nurses, midwives, community public health nurses and social workers to recognise discrimination and to challenge it where it occurs. Professional practice means each person is responsible for what they do. It is no excuse to say, 'I don't know what to do'. The codes of conduct for each profession define what a professional must do.

Activity 20

Linking to P5 and M2.

Pick three of the following examples. Then:
- identify the type of discrimination, either direct or indirect
- explain the basis for the discrimination. For example, is it age or race or disability?
- say what you as a nurse or social worker can do to challenge the discrimination, what difficulties you may encounter and how you would overcome those difficulties

A is 14 years old and admitted to hospital in labour. One of the carers suggests that the girl has been sleeping around.

B is admitted to Casualty with bruising and broken ribs, having been beaten by her husband. She is Asian. The student nurse working with you says, 'They are all the same, those foreigners.'

C is admitted to Casualty following a road traffic accident. He tells the ward clerk he is HIV positive. She has strong views on homosexuality and makes a comment that 'It is his own fault he got HIV.'

D is about to be admitted to a care home. The care manager finds out that he is gay and refuses to accept him.

E is recovering in hospital from a broken leg. He needs physiotherapy but is told he is too old because he is 70.

F is discharged from hospital into a care home. F is vegetarian and Hindu. She is not offered a vegetarian option at meal times so ends up having bread and butter or potatoes.

Personal beliefs and value systems

We are all human beings and have been influenced by our culture, beliefs and life events. Sometimes we accept the beliefs and values of our parents, but sometimes we examine them and find we cannot agree with them. Each person is entitled to their own beliefs and values, but a health and social care professional must not let their beliefs influence the care they give.

Case Study

Kaz was brought up in a working-class family. People expressed their views openly. Her dad lost his job when the local factory closed down and resented the fact that the Sikh family next door always seemed to have plenty of money. He assumed they were all scroungers on benefits and said so to his mates down the pub.

When Kaz was 18, she got a job as a care assistant at the local care home and was surprised to see the woman from next door working there. They got chatting and Kaz learned that Mr Singh worked as a bus driver and left for work at 4am. He also had a part-time job as a porter at the local hospital. That explained why they always seemed to have a new car and nice things.

Kaz mentioned this to her dad and suggested he might try for a job at the hospital. He got angry and said he wasn't a porter. He was a skilled craftsman and wasn't going to turn his hand to such work. Jobseeker's allowance was enough for him.

Next time he went on about the scroungers next door, Kaz was quiet. She knew how hard Mr Singh worked. She loved her dad, but she could see that he was wrong about Mr Singh.

A few months later, Kaz's dad fell over on his way home from the pub and broke his leg. He found it difficult to use his crutches and was stuck in the house. Kaz told Mrs Singh at work and the next day Mr Singh came round to ask whether he could do anything to help. Mrs Singh came too and brought them some home-made vegetable soup. At first Kaz's dad didn't want to let them in, but Kaz asked them in. Next day Mr Singh offered to take Kaz's dad to the hospital for his check-up.

Kaz's dad never really accepted his neighbours, but Kaz began to see them as people. When she started her nursing course, she had a good understanding of some of the Sikh customs and even knew that Mr Singh's wife was called Kaur, not Singh.

Kaz changed from being prejudiced to seeing people as individuals. Not everyone changes their beliefs, but professionals in health and social care must be self-aware, tolerant of differences and non-judgemental in their practice. Legal, ethical and policy guidelines say what professionals should do, but unless they are really committed to the care value base, they will not be anti-discriminatory.

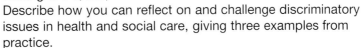

Activity 21

Linking to P6, M3, D2.
Describe how you can reflect on and challenge discriminatory issues in health and social care, giving three examples from practice.
Analyse how your personal beliefs and value systems may influence your anti-discriminatory practice.
Evaluate three practical strategies to reconcile your beliefs and values with anti-discriminatory practice in health and social care. To what extent are the strategies effective – wholly, partly, or not at all?

SUMMARY

- Diversity has numerous benefits to society.

- There are many ways equality and diversity can be promoted within health and social care settings.

- Individuals have a number of rights when receiving health and social care services.

- Discrimination can occur on an individual basis or through sections of society.

- Discriminatory practice may be displayed in different ways. The effects can be short term or long term and can affect people in different ways.

- Conventions, legislation and regulations promote anti-discriminatory practice.

- In health and social care settings, anti-discriminatory practice is actively promoted through the setting of standards for the conduct, performance and ethics of sector workers.

- Personal belief and value systems may influence an individual's anti-discriminatory practice.

Grading grid

In order to pass this unit, the evidence that the learner presents for assessment needs to demonstrate that they can meet all of the learning outcomes for the unit. The criteria for a pass grade describe the level of achievement required to pass this unit.

GRADING CRITERIA

TO ACHIEVE A PASS GRADE THE EVIDENCE MUST SHOW THAT THE LEARNER IS ABLE TO:	TO ACHIEVE A MERIT GRADE THE EVIDENCE MUST SHOW THAT, IN ADDITION TO THE PASS CRITERIA, THE LEARNER IS ABLE TO:	TO ACHIEVE A DISTINCTION GRADE THE EVIDENCE MUST SHOW THAT, IN ADDITION TO THE PASS AND MERIT CRITERIA, THE LEARNER IS ABLE TO:
P1 explain the benefits of diversity to society		
P2 use recognised terminology to explain the importance of promoting equality, recognising diversity and respecting rights in health and social care settings		
P3 explain the potential effects of discriminatory practice on those who use health or social care services		
P4 describe how legislation, codes of practice, rules of conduct, charters and organisational policies are used to promote anti-discriminatory practice	M1 explain the influences of a recent or emerging national policy development on organisational policy with regard to anti-discriminatory practice	D1 evaluate how a recent or emerging policy development influences organisational and personal practice in relation to anti-discriminatory practice
P5 explain how those working in health and social care settings can actively promote anti-discriminatory practice	M2 explain difficulties that may be encountered when implementing anti-discriminatory practice	

GRADING CRITERIA

TO ACHIEVE A PASS GRADE THE EVIDENCE MUST SHOW THAT THE LEARNER IS ABLE TO:	TO ACHIEVE A MERIT GRADE THE EVIDENCE MUST SHOW THAT, IN ADDITION TO THE PASS CRITERIA, THE LEARNER IS ABLE TO:	TO ACHIEVE A DISTINCTION GRADE THE EVIDENCE MUST SHOW THAT, IN ADDITION TO THE PASS AND MERIT CRITERIA, THE LEARNER IS ABLE TO:
P6 describe ways of reflecting on and challenging discriminatory issues in health and social care.	M3 analyse how personal beliefs and value systems may influence own anti-discriminatory practice.	D2 evaluate practical strategies to reconcile own beliefs and values with anti-discriminatory practice in health and social care.

This unit looks at how to promote health, safety and security in health and social care settings. Health and social care settings frequently present potential hazards which can pose a threat to the health and wellbeing of service users, staff, visitors and others.

Learning Outcomes

On completion of this unit you should be able to:

1 Understand potential hazards in health and social care
2 Understand how legislation, guidelines, policies and procedures promote health, safety and security
3 Understand roles and responsibilities for health, safety and security in health and social care settings
4 Know how to deal with hazards in a local environment

KEY CONCEPTS

A **hazard** is something that can cause harm.

A **risk** is the effect of a hazard and the probability of a hazard occurring.

1 Understand potential hazards in health and social care

Hazards

There are many possible hazards within health and social care environments. Hazards that may occur within a health and social care setting can have numerous causes. They may be the result of the working environment, such as poor working conditions, including bad lighting, equipment that is not properly maintained or substances that you might have to use (such as bleach), or of incidents such as challenging behaviour from service users.

Remember

Your working environment might not just be your health and social care setting; it can also be out in the community, in service users' homes or in the premises of another organisation. You will not have as much control over hazards in these environments.

Activity 1

Look at the picture below.

1 What hazards can you spot?
2 What would be the consequences of these?
3 What could you do to reduce the risk?

Working environment

Hazards may arise within the working environment. Poor staff training or the environment itself could lead to risks to service users, staff and property.

Working practices

These are activities that you carry out every day within your working life. During these practices, you may come across some things that can present hazards, including day-to-day activities such as craft activities or cooking, or improper use of equipment.

Incidents

These are events that may occur within your workplace. It is not always possible to plan for these as they may include intruders or aggressive and dangerous occurrences involving service users. Other possible incidents include bomb scares or chemical spillages. However, your employer should have policies and procedures for what to do in the event of these emergencies.

Fire is one example of an incident. Policies and procedures within the workplace should minimise the risk of this occurring. It is far easier to prevent a fire happening than to address the consequences.

Risks

A risk is what may happen as a consequence of the hazard. This can include injury or harm to the service users, staff, relatives or other people who are present at the time. (This can include professionals or members of the public.) There is a possibility that people may be put in danger or there may be damage to the environment or equipment. Certain practices may put people at risk of illness or infection.

Accidents

Vulnerable service users may be at risk of accidents. Although this could be as a result of the hazards already identified, it could be because of the vulnerability of the service user themselves, perhaps because of sensory impairment, disability or frailty.

2 Understand how legislation, guidelines, policies and procedures promote health, safety and security

Legislation, policies and procedures exist to promote a safer working environment and reduce the potential for risks occurring.

Health and Safety at Work Act 1974

This is the main piece of British health and safety law and has led to the development of many other pieces of health and safety legislation. It sets out the general duties that employers have to their workers and to any public that might enter the premises. It also lists the responsibilities employees have to themselves and to each other.

The main part of the Act requires employers to carry out risk assessments and to appoint a person responsible for health and safety in the workplace.

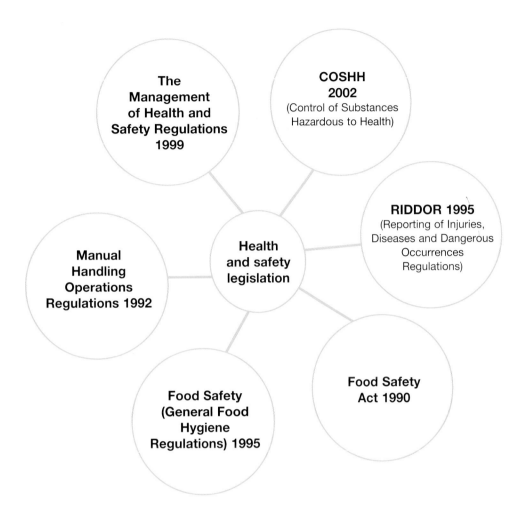

KEY CONCEPTS

Regulations are laws approved by parliament.

Employers' responsibilities include:

- so far as it is reasonably practicable, to ensure your health, safety and welfare at work
- to consult employees or their safety representative on matters relating to health and safety at work
- to carry out risk assessments or implement measures as identified in the assessment
- to report certain injuries, diseases and dangerous occurrences

Employees' responsibilities include:

- taking reasonable care for their own health and safety and that of others
- cooperating with their employer on health and safety
- correctly using work items provided by their employers
- not interfering with or misusing anything provided for their health, safety and welfare

(*source*: HSE)

Activity 2

Every workplace should display the health and safety law poster and appoint a person responsible for health and safety. Within your work placement, locate the poster, find out who your health and safety representative is and write down some of the responsibilities your employer and the employees have.

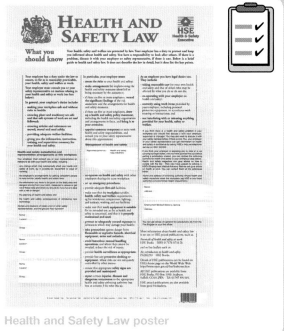

Health and Safety Law poster

KEY CONCEPTS

Manual handling involves lifting or moving objects or people without a mechanical aid or equipment.

Manual Handling Regulations 1992

The Manual Handling Regulations aim to reduce the risk of injury from lifting or moving objects or people. This may include lifting, lowering, pushing, pulling or carrying.

Activity 3

Within your placement or a general health and social care setting, answer the following questions:

● Who might be injured from poor manual handling?
● For each of the people you have identified, what parts of the body would be damaged from poor manual handling?
● What would be the consequences of this? Think of the whole person (physical, intellectual, emotional and social) and the working environment.

Working with a partner, discuss why correct manual handling procedures are so important.

These regulations provide information for both employers and employees. The main principle is that you should avoid any manual handling if it is at all possible. An example of this would mean using a hoist rather than carrying someone yourself.

If it is not possible to avoid manual handling altogether, it is important that the risk of injury is assessed. This would mean looking at the whole job that is to be undertaken and deciding who might get injured, why this might occur and the impact that this potential injury would have. Generally, most manual handling injuries that occur could have been avoided. The risks that have been identified should then be reduced as much as possible (*source:* HSE).

Activity 4

Why would an employee be able to assist with manual handling assessments? What expertise could they offer?

Reflect

Within health and social care a hoist can be used to move people. As well as reducing the risk of injury it is more professional. Why do you think this is? (Think of the rights of service users and the care value base.) Any equipment used should also be maintained and employers should train staff so that they know how to use the equipment safely.

Although this assessment is an employer's responsibility, an employee has responsibilities and can assist in carrying out the risk assessment.

Employees' responsibilities include following any structures in place to assist with manual handling and cooperating with their employer. Employees also have a responsibility to inform their employer if there are any hazardous handling activities and to ensure that they do not put others at risk.

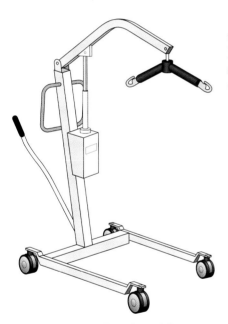

Hoist used in health and social care settings

Activity 5

You are working at Rose Cottage Nursing Home. Derek needs a bath, an occasion on which you would normally use a hoist. Your two colleagues say, 'Oh, I can't be bothered using that, it's in another room. Let's just lift him.'

How would you react to this situation? What could you say to ensure that he is handled appropriately? Do you envisage any difficulties in tackling this issue?

If you do have to lift, the appropriate manual handling work should be undertaken. In a care setting, you will often be involved in helping people to move. It is important that this is done safely. Often people can present a hazard themselves. Think of the clothes they may wear. For example, a service user who is wearing a long dressing gown may present a trip hazard to staff or service users.

COSHH 2002

COSHH stands for Control of Substances Hazardous to Health. This covers using, storing and disposing of any substances. The basis of this Act is that employers should assess the risk that hazardous substances can present and then take precautions to minimise the risk.

The Act provides eight basic principles which should be followed:

- Assess the risk – who might be harmed and how severely?
- Decide what precautions are necessary – what needs to be in place as a preventative measure?
- Prevent or control exposure – this is putting into place the precautions.
- Ensure control measures are used – check regularly that the workplace is using measures in place.
- Monitor exposure – ensure workplaces are not being subjected to high levels of harmful substances.
- Carry out health surveillance.
- Plan to deal with emergencies – provide guidance on what to do in the event of an emergency.
- Train and inform employees – train new employees and update staff as necessary.

(*source*: HSE)

The Act also looks at storage, labelling and disposal of substances. Substances should be stored correctly (for example, not putting these in an area where children may be able to gain access), labelled properly (for example, not putting bleach in a lemonade bottle) and disposed of (how would employees dispose of substances?).

There are many hazardous substances that you may use in health and social care. As well as the more obvious medical ones, everyday items such as bleach, washing-up liquid and soup are covered. Your health and social care setting should have COSHH information for all of these substances. Workers then have a responsibility to follow these risk assessments. COSHH regulations will inform workers of any protective equipment that they may need to use.

Hazard signs

Some products will display hazard signs such as those below. This provides additional warning for these chemicals.

Extremely or Highly Flammable

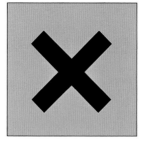

Harmful or Irritant

Corrosive

Activity 6

Your work placement should have a COSHH file which contains risk assessments on using any hazardous products. Ask whether your workplace has one and make a list of any of the substances used within it.

RIDDOR 1995

This legislation covers injuries, certain diseases and dangerous occurrences. These events must be recorded and may be reported to the Health and Safety Executive (HSE). In the case of serious accidents the HSE will investigate.

Incidents reportable under the regulations include the following:

- death or major injury of an employee on the premises or if an injury that occurs within the workplace results in the employee being off work for three or more days
- diseases – certain diseases are also reportable.
- dangerous occurrences – incidents that have happened but did not result in a reportable injury. An example includes electrical short circuit or explosion.

(*source:* HSE)

Accident book

RIDDOR (Reporting of Injuries, Diseases and Dangerous Occurrences Regulations) 1995 requires all workplaces to keep a record of all accidents or near accidents. An accident book record should include the date, time and place, who was involved, what happened, any injury and then action taken. Confidential details such as address should be recorded separately. Under the Data Protection Act, accident books now have a detached sheet, i.e. they are not kept confidential. Accidents should be reviewed every so often to identify how they could be prevented in the future. The RIDDOR regulations require the workplace to notify the HSE of any occupational injury that occurs. This could be a death, reportable injuries such as a fracture, certain diseases or dangerous occurrences.

Once reported, an accident will be investigated and the enforcing authority can advise on further preventative measures. It is also important that accidents are recorded in case of legal implications.

Activity 7

Look at this example of an accident form.

Accident Form
Name: Jodie Case
Address: 121 Accident Street, A11 5LG
~~Male~~/Female
Age: 65
Date of Birth: 01.01.1943

Date and Time of Treatment: 2.5.07 2.50pm
State Specific Injury and Location on Body: Scald to left hand
Details of Treatment Given: Ran under cold water, medical advice sought

Signature (first aider): Barry Aider
Date: 2.5.07

Details of Incident (give as much detail as you can, including location, date and time): Jodie was making herself a cup of tea. As she leaned over her mug to put the tea back in the cupboard, she knocked over her cup of tea, some of which went on her left hand. It took place in the kitchen 2.5.07 at 2.45pm.

Signature (injured person): Jodie Case
Signature (first aider): Barry Aider

Activity 7 (continued)

Now fill in your own accident form.

Name:
Address:
Male/Female
Age:
Date of Birth:

Date and Time of Treatment:
State Specific Injury and Location on Body:
Details of Treatment Given:

Signature (first aider):
Date:

Details of Incident (give as much detail as you can, including location, date and time):

Signature (injured person):
Signature (first aider):

Activity 8

What control measures are in place in your setting to reduce the risk from poor food hygiene?

Food Safety Act 1990

Within a health and social care setting workers must ensure that they do not cause food to be dangerous to health and also must keep good food hygiene within the workplace.

Food safety (general food hygiene regulations)

This is all about managing food hygiene, identifying the risks and what could go wrong and then bringing in checks and controls to ensure that any risk is reduced.

The Management of Health and Safety at Work Regulations 1999

These regulations state that employers have a responsibility to train staff in health and safety. This is in relation to all the major points of the legislation so would include preventing fire, controlling the spread of infection, moving and handling appropriately. It also requires employers to carry out risk assessments.

Organisational policy and procedures

Each workplace will have policies and procedures which state what the employer has done and what employees should do to maintain health and safety. They will reflect the health and safety legislation.

Activity 9

Relates to P3, M1, D1.
Find out what your organisation's policies and procedures are.
● Which legislations do they reflect?
● How do these legislations work in practice?
● How effective are they in promoting health, safety and security?

3 Understand roles and responsibilities for health, safety and security in health and social care settings

The HSE, employers and employees have responsibilities to help maintain a healthy workforce.

The HSE is responsible for enforcing health and safety laws. HSE inspectors visit the workplace to make sure that the legislation is being followed. Although they do have a role in investigating accidents or complaints, they generally work helping workplaces to interpret and put into action health and safety legislation. The HSE does have powers to enforce legislation not being followed, however.

Employers have the responsibility to keep employees informed about health and safety. This entails providing training and necessary equipment and informing employees of their roles and responsibilities.

Employees have the role of following procedures and notifying their employer of any extra measures that need to be in place or if something is not working. If employees are aware of a problem they have a responsibility to discuss it with the employer or, in the case of some larger organisations, to discuss it with a safety representative.

Activity 10

During one day at placement make a list of anything that you or other people do that helps maintain a healthy and safe workplace. You may come up with some of the following:
● dealt with spilling of hazardous or non-hazardous substances
● followed correct manual handling procedures
● reported health and safety issues to the appropriate people
● checked the identity of people entering the building
● disposed of waste immediately and safely
● identified a potential health, safety or security risk and reported accordingly
● completed a health and safety record

As health and safety are protected by law, some of the responsibilities are determined by law. Each organisation will have policies that should also be followed.

RESPONSIBILITIES	EMPLOYER	EMPLOYEE
Risk assessment (examination of what may cause harm to people)	To examine the workplace and identify what may cause harm, to whom and how to minimise the risk. To inform employees of risk assessment	To follow risk assessment procedures in place and to notify employer of any changes
Monitoring of working practices	To put measures in place to monitor workplace and practices	To follow working practices and inform employers of any changes
Storing equipment	To provide guidance on how to store equipment and materials and the means to carry this out	To follow policy and procedure and store equipment and materials appropriately
Dealing with hazardous and non-hazardous materials	To provide risk assessments, policies and procedures on how to use these substances. Train workers to use them	To follow policies and procedures. To clear up spillages according to risk assessments
Manual handling	To assess the risks and reduce the need for manual handling. To train workers in manual handling	To follow manual handling procedures and report any faults with equipment
Reporting health and safety issues	To report major accidents to the HSE	To report any issues to your employer or representative
Completing health and safety and security records	To keep all records, such as risk assessments, up to date	To keep all records up to date and confidential. These may include accident books

Examples of responsibilities (relates to P4)

There are other responsibilities to do with health and safety, including checking rights of entry. This will assist service users to feel safe within their homes. Employers should have procedures on how to do this which employees should follow. Employees should be aware of the security measures within their workplace. For example, some workplaces have swipe card entry or provide identity cards which employees should wear. Workers should not allow people they do not know or who have not provided sufficient identification onto the premises.

It is important that an employee operates only within the limits of their role and does not undertake an activity that they do not feel confident in doing. You should follow these procedures, take care not to misuse anything, ensure your health and safety, and tell your employer about anything that might impact upon people's health and safety.

Activity 11

Which of the following accidents will be your fault and which will be the fault of your employer?

● Your manual handling policy has not been updated and you have hurt your back.
● You go to work with a hangover and as you are not concentrating, you cause an accident.
● You have known for some time a hoist is not working. You say nothing. Someone has an accident.
● After you have told your employer about the hoist, your employer does nothing.
● You missed health and safety training day as you were sick. You are expected to carry on as normal.
● After you have been on the training day you decide not to bother with a hoist as it saves time.

Remember

If you have been given training and you do not follow it, you will be responsible for any consequences.

Activity 12

Relating to P4.
Talk to your health and safety representative at college or on placement. Use this information and your staff handbook to make a list of your responsibilities.
List them under the headings of the relevant pieces of legislation.

4 Know how to deal with hazards in a local environment

Some service users, such as children, older people or those in residential care, may go out of their environment and enter another one. This can therefore pose an additional health, safety and security risk as you have less control over this environment. Possible trips include going to a park, playground or cinema, going shopping or going swimming.

Often before taking a service user into the environment you should undertake a risk assessment and survey of the area. This will ensure that you know the layout of the area and where the toilets are, etc. It also means you can be prepared for taking vulnerable people out into the community itself. By being prepared you can minimise the possibility of risks within the area. This may include injury or harm to service users. Service users may abscond or may not feel confident in meeting and mixing with strangers. In addition, vulnerable service users may present a risk to the public. Service users with challenging behaviour may on occasion be aggressive towards members of the public.

There are additional dangers that will present themselves outside only, such as traffic accidents and fires. While many of these you cannot account for, being familiar with an area and preparing yourself as much as you can will minimise the risk. A risk assessment not only forms part of the legislation but is integral to minimising the possibility of accidents.

Survey

Before you take vulnerable service users into a local environment, it is good practice to survey the area. This will enable you to prepare an adequate risk assessment and to check the facilities available. You may work with a service user who has an aversion to dogs, for example. If the local pub you are taking them to has a dog, it will not be a good plan!

When surveying an area you should consider health, safety and security risks.

- Health – will the environment pose any risk to a person's health? For example, high-pollen areas may attract bees. This should be a consideration if a person has an allergy.
- Safety – is the area safe? Is there a litter problem? If there is any equipment, is it in working order?
- Security – does the area pose any security risks?

Minimising the risks

You may have to undertake certain things to minimise the risks of hazards to service users. An example may be to include extra staff. You may also show staff the area before taking service users into it so they know what to expect. You may like to undertake work with service users to prepare them for what they are doing.

Once the risk has been thoroughly investigated, you can make recommendations and then put these into action.

Risks

There are numerous possible risks from going to a local environment. Take going to a park, for example (see figure opposite).

Activity 13

Think of another environment, possibly one you take service users to. List the risks within that setting.

Risk assessment

A risk assessment is an investigation into what can cause harm to people. The reason for doing this is to ensure that no one gets hurt. It also fulfils a legal requirement. The Health and Safety Executive provides five steps to risk assessment. They are shown below, with information and an example.

STEP AND EXPLANATION	EXAMPLE (WALKING TO THE SHOPS)
1 LOOK FOR HAZARDS What can cause harm? If you are unsure, ask others or look at previous accident book records	The following could cause harm: ● crossing the road ● slips, trips and falls ● being in the community
2 DECIDE WHO MIGHT BE HARMED AND HOW Don't forget that some groups or individuals may be more at risk of harm than others	The service user could be involved in a road traffic incident or damage property. Those with particular illnesses may be at risk due to their illness (e.g. someone with epilepsy may have a fit). The service user is at risk of absconding and is vulnerable from other members of the public
3 EVALUATE THE RISK AND DECIDE WHETHER EXISTING PRECAUTIONS ARE ADEQUATE OR WHETHER MORE SHOULD BE DONE Here you are looking at how you can minimise the risk	Many of the precautions are already in place, such as taking medication for service users with specific conditions, or ensuring vehicles are roadworthy to minimise risk of road traffic incidents
4 RECORD YOUR FINDINGS	You could carry out risk assessments with the service user (or advocate). This gives them control over their own lives and independence. Risk assessments should be dated and should demonstrate where checks have been made and how hazards have been addressed
5 REVIEW ASSESSMENT	Hazards and risks may change, so it is good practice to review and change if necessary

Five steps to risk assessment

An example of a risk assessment is shown below. This encompasses the general identification of a risk, then assessing it for the risks it may present to a patient or service user, the workers and the public, then looking at how these can be minimised. This risk assessment should then be dated and reviewed to see where improvements can be made.

Activity	Hazard	Hazard rating	Control measures in place	Likeli-hood	Hazard x likelihood	Assessed by	Review date
Walking to the park	Road traffic accidents	3	1:1 supervision. Only one road to cross. Staff and service users to follow highway code	1	3		6 mths
	Slips, trips and falls	2	Do not go if icy. Wear sensible footwear	1	2		6 mths
	Service user absconding	3	Adequate supervision. Carry mobile phone and contact numbers	1	3		6 mths

Example of a risk assessment

Activity 14

Pick an activity that you may do now or wish to do in the future. Carry out a risk assessment on this.

Generally hazards are rated on a scale of 1–3 depending on the severity. Likelihood is also on a 1–3 scale (1 = unlikely). The chances are then the two multiplied together. If the risk is 3 or less than 3, then the activity is safe to carry out. Any more, then further action to reduce the risks would be necessary.

First aid procedures

First aid should protect you, the first aider, and the casualty. The principles of first aid are basic:

- to preserve life
- to limit the effect of the condition
- to promote recovery

When dealing with a first aid situation, whether minor or severe, certain qualities and skills are very valuable and will help you to deal with these situations.

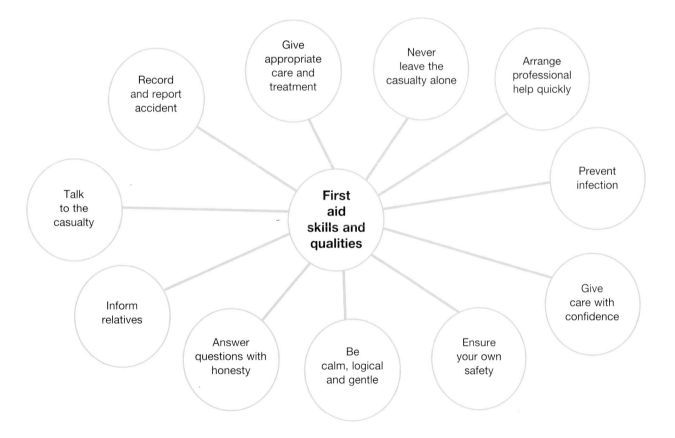

Remember

As a first aider you may be faced with several jobs at once, for example telephoning, giving aid, maintaining safety. Bystanders and onlookers can be useful in giving assistance, but always make sure they are given correct and clear instructions.

Activity 15

Read the following statements. As a first aider dealing with an emergency, put them in logical order. Decide why you have put them in this order.

1 Make area safe
2 Give emergency aid
3 Get help
4 Deal with aftermath
5 Prioritise the casualties
6 Record and report
7 Assess situation

Answer: 7,1,5,2,3,6,4

Activity 16

With a partner, find the radial pulse (wrist). Find the carotid pulse (neck).
Sit your partner in a comfortable position to observe respirations (breathing in and out = 1 respiration).
Count and record these findings for a full minute and compare them against the norms below:

- Normal range – pulse 60–80 beats per minute (adults)
- Normal range – respirations 16–20 per minute (adults)

With your partner, discuss why your findings may be above or below the normal range.

- Do you smoke?
- Have you just done some exercise?
- Are you feeling well?
- Is your environment hot or cold?
- Do you suffer from a medical condition which may affect your findings?

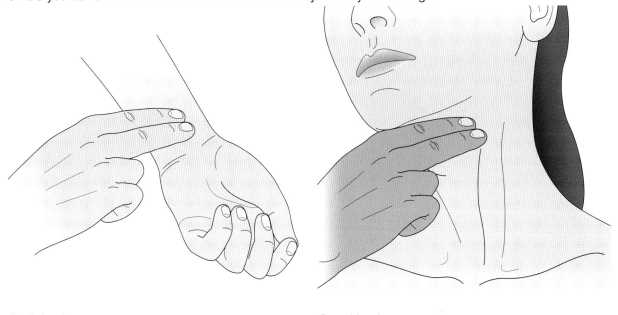

Radial pulse   Carotid pulse

Bleeding

Did you know?

Some professional sports men and women have extremely efficient cardiovascular systems and their pulse rate may be around 40 beats per minute.

Loss of fluid from the body causes a reduction in blood pressure. If not controlled this can cause shock and may be fatal, so it is important to control bleeding. Any open wound will allow germs to enter the body and cause infection, so action should always be quick and hygienic.

Severe bleeding is loss of blood from a major artery. It will pump out under great pressure and appear bright red as it is oxygen rich. Loss of blood from a major vein will gush out and appear darker in colour as it has given up oxygen to carry carbon dioxide.

What will the casualty look like?

As the casualty is losing a large amount of blood they may be pale and sweating, and experiencing rapid breathing and pain (see shock box below).

Treatment

Lay the casualty down and make them comfortable. Control bleeding by direct pressure with a sterile dressing, wearing gloves if possible. Raise and support the affected area (as far as the casualty is comfortable). Keep them warm if you suspect shock. Check the bandage for further bleeding. If you see seepage, apply another one.

If the casualty is still bleeding, re-do the bandaging and apply a new dressing, ensuring correct positioning. Arrange transfer to hospital (999).

CAUSES	SIGNS AND SYMPTOMS	TREATMENT
Major blood loss	Cold, clammy skin	Deal with the cause, i.e. bleeding
Severe burns	Pale	Reassure and comfort
Heart attack	Nausea	Keep warm
Severe diarrhoea	Thirst	Lie down
Anaphylaxis	Rapid breathing	Raise feet if comfortable
Drug overdose	Rapid, weak pulse	Do not allow food, drink, cigarettes
Hypoglycaemia	Dizziness	Transfer to hospital
Hyperglycaemia	Blue tinge around mouth	Observe vital signs
Severe emotional upset	Aggressive behaviour	
	Unconsciousness	

The shock box

Do not allow the casualty to eat, drink or smoke, in case they require an anaesthetic on arrival at hospital. Also they may faint as they take in nicotine rather than important oxygen, lose consciousness and inhale gastric contents.

Complications

If an object is embedded in the wound you should:

- not remove it – it may be preventing major bleeding
- control the bleeding with direct pressure around the object

- gently cover and protect it
- raise the injured area – make sure casualty is comfortable
- arrange transfer to hospital (999)

Activity 17

Match the descriptions with the wound types.

TYPE	DESCRIPTION
1 Incised wound	A Jagged wound edges – high risk of infection
2 Laceration	B Small entry site, large exit site if found – high possibility of internal damage
3 Abrasion (graze)	C Straight wound edges – high risk of infection
4 Contusion (bruise)	D Small entry site – high risk of internal damage
5 Puncture wound	E Damage to small blood vessels under skin
6 Gunshot wound	F Superficial damage to small blood vessels – high risk of infection

Answers
1C, 2A, 3F, 4E, 5D, 6B

Minor bleeding

This is from a capillary near to the surface of the skin and may bleed freely at first but usually stops quickly with direct pressure. The wound should be cleaned and covered to prevent infections. Check tetanus immunisation – if over ten years ago, casualty will need another one from a GP or hospital.

Internal bleeding

This may follow an injury or accident or happen spontaneously (bleeding ulcer). It can be serious, as a build-up of blood internally can cause pressure on major organs, for example brain, heart, lungs, causing further damage.

What will the casualty look like?

They will display signs of pain, anxiety, shock (see shock box). Bleeding may occur from the nearest body opening (orifice), for example:

- bleeding from the stomach – vomit may contain blood
- bleeding in the skull – blood may trickle from ears and nose
- bleeding in the bowel – blood may be seen in the stools (faeces)

If the casualty has been injured, a bruised area may appear over the internally bleeding site. This is called 'pattern bleeding'.

Activity 18

Visit www.bbc. co.uk/health/first_ai d_action and click onto **bleeding**. Then follow the activity and take the 999 challenge.

Treatment

Reassure the casualty. Treat them for shock. Arrange transfer to hospital (999). Record and report vital signs. Don't leave the casualty alone.

Complications

Early diagnosis and treatment of internal bleeding are important because a casualty who collapses with signs of shock and no visible signs of bleeding could die.

Fracture

This is a break or crack in a bone. Young bones may splinter or bend, causing a 'greenstick fracture'. Older bones may break more easily from accidents or diseases.

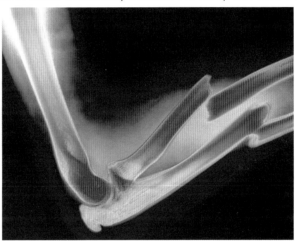

Fractures can be:

- stable – the broken ends of the bone do not move as they are forced together or they may not be completely broken. Example: wrist, hip, ankles, feet as in David Beckham's famous metatarsal injury
- unstable – bones can move out of line and could cause damage to tissues, nerves and surrounding blood vessels
- open – one of the ends of the broken bone punctures the skin and can be seen externally
- closed – the skin is not broken but internal damage may still happen
- direct – this is when a fracture occurs from direct external force, for example a kick to the leg
- indirect – this occurs away from the site of impact. For example, if someone falls and puts out their hand to cushion the fall, a fracture may occur in the shoulder or collar bone

What will the casualty look like?

They may experience pain, swelling and bruising at the injury site, and difficulty in moving the limb or surrounding area. The casualty may have heard a cracking sound, or the limb may be shortened or distorted, for example in an unstable hip fracture. Bone may be sticking out and there could be signs and symptoms of shock – see shock box.

Treatment

All casualties should be transferred to hospital for correct diagnosis and professional treatment. The first aider should:

- make the casualty comfortable, keeping them as still as possible
- stop the injured area from moving, using support from bandages above and below the fracture site
- not allow casualty to eat, drink or smoke as they may need an anaesthetic

Complications

Watch out for signs and symptoms of shock (see shock box) as an unstable fracture may have caused internal bleeding, for example fractured ribs. Keep the open wound clean as there is a risk of infection. Any bandages you apply may become tight from swelling in the area, so keep checking the injury site.

For different types of bandaging see *First Aid Manual* by Dorling Kindersley, authorised manual of St John Ambulance, St Andrews Ambulance Association and the British Red Cross. Using the suggested scenarios at the end of this section, practise some of the bandages displayed in the above manual.

Sprain

This is injury or damage to a ligament. A ligament is the fibrous tissue that connects bones to bones and holds your skeleton together. If a ligament is overstretched out of position, this is called a sprain. Common sprain sites are ankles, wrists and knees. It is often caused in sports activities.

What will the casualty look like?

There will be pain, swelling and redness at the site of injury. The casualty may be unable to use the area or may have restricted movement.

Treatment

The following mnemonic will help you remember the treatment for sprains and strains:
R – Rest the injured area.
I – Apply ice or cold compress to the area.
C – Compress or bandage the area.
E – Elevate the injured area, making sure the casualty is comfortable.

Complications

If this treatment does not help, the casualty should seek medical advice as it may be a fracture.

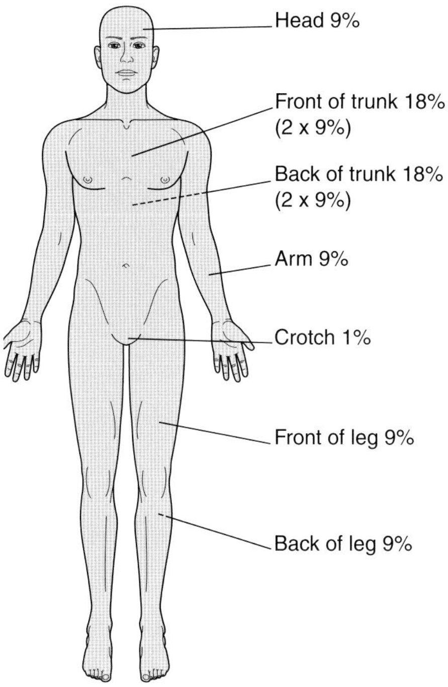
Head 9%
Front of trunk 18% (2 x 9%)
Back of trunk 18% (2 x 9%)
Arm 9%
Crotch 1%
Front of leg 9%
Back of leg 9%
Rule of nines

Burns and scalds

Burns are assessed by the depth of skin damage as well as how much surface area has been affected:

- superficial – outer layer of skin, e.g. from sunburn or a minor domestic injury
- partial thickness – affects the outer layer, may be red, blistered and extremely painful
- full thickness – this is often pain free due to nerve damage; the skin may look pale, charred or waxy

A common way to assess the extent of burns is 'the rule of nines'. Rule of nines relates to the percentage of the body affected by the burn. It is a quick way of estimating the surface area that is affected.

In children, the head is more than 9% of the body and a good way of estimating burns is to say the child's palm is 1% of the body's surface area. Other percentages are:

- Face and scalp 9% (18% for a child)
- Back 18%
- Perineum 1%
- Arm each 9%
- Front 18% (trunk)
- Upper arm each 9%
- Lower leg each 9%

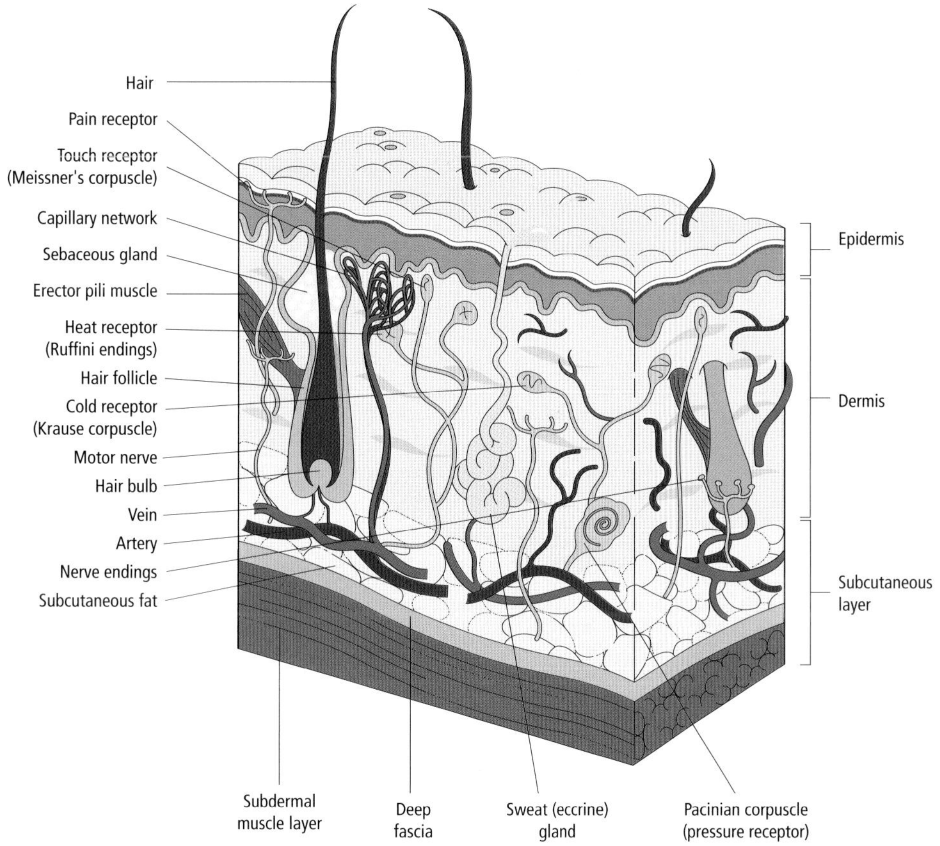
Hair
Pain receptor
Touch receptor (Meissner's corpuscle)
Capillary network
Sebaceous gland
Erector pili muscle
Heat receptor (Ruffini endings)
Hair follicle
Cold receptor (Krause corpuscle)
Motor nerve
Hair bulb
Vein
Artery
Nerve endings
Subcutaneous fat
Epidermis
Dermis
Subcutaneous layer
Subdermal muscle layer
Deep fascia
Sweat (eccrine) gland
Pacinian corpuscle (pressure receptor)
Structure of the skin

What will the casualty look like?

Due to loss of body fluid the casualty may have signs of shock (see shock box on page 65). Depending on the depth of the burn the skin may be red, swollen and blistered; it may also be very painful.

Treatment

You need to stop the burning sensation, so move the casualty away from the heated area. Reassure the casualty and make them comfortable. Immerse the area in cold water or other cold fluids for at least ten minutes or until the burning sensation stops. Keep the area as clean as possible as there is a high risk of infection. Remove any rings or metals as they may retain heat and restrict circulation. Cover injured area with a sterile, non-fluffy dressing if possible.

Seek medical help if:

- casualty is suffering signs of shock
- the burn involves face, hands, feet or genitals
- they are all full-thickness burns
- they are partial thickness and more than 1 per cent (same size as casualty's palm)
- they are superficial and more than 5 per cent (five of casualty's palms)
- they are burns of mixed thickness.

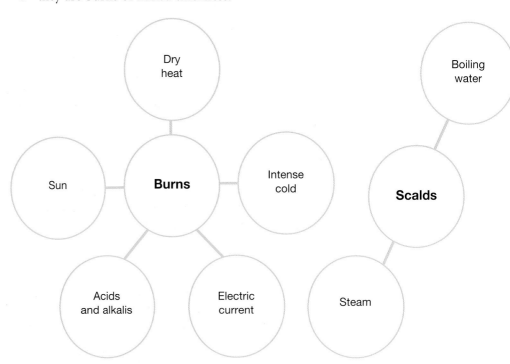

Causes of burns and scalds

Activity 19

Go to www.bbc.
co.uk/health/first_ai
d_action.
Click on 'essential
skills', then 'burns
and scald', and take
the interactive test.

Complications

Infection is a big risk, so *do not*:

- pop any blisters
- remove clothing stuck to the burn
- apply lotions, creams or fat to the burn
- overcool the area.

Asthma

Asthma is a respiratory (breathing) condition. It causes the casualty to have difficulty in breathing, particularly expiration (breathing out). The reason the airways become narrowed is usually because they are irritated by 'triggers' (see list below of possible triggers). The muscles around the wall of the airway tighten and the inside of the airway becomes swollen and produces mucus.

Possible triggers are:

- animal fur
- smoke fumes
- dust
- exercise
- emotional onset

What will the casualty look like?

They will probably have obvious breathing difficulties, particularly breathing out when they may 'wheeze'. They may be agitated or panicky. They may cough and find it difficult to speak. If the attack has lasted a few minutes without medication, they may be pale as the oxygen levels in their body are decreasing. They may have a blue tinge around their mouth.

Treatment

Calm the casualty down and reassure them. Advise them to take their inhaler if they have one. Sit them in a comfortable position in a well-ventilated room. Remove them from the 'trigger' (if possible).

Complications

After three minutes, if they do not feel any relief the casualty should take another dose from their inhaler. After five minutes, if there is no effect or if their condition is getting worse, arrange transfer to hospital. Keep giving doses of inhaler until 999 arrives.

If this is their first asthma attack, take them to hospital.

If the casualty loses consciousness, see page 75 for recovery position and prepare to deliver CPR – asthma can be fatal.

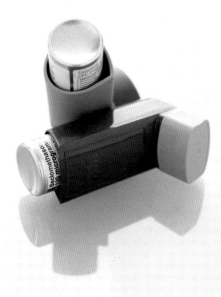

Inhalers

Types of inhaler

- Reliever inhaler (blue cap) – used in an attack.
- Preventer inhaler (brown cap) – used each day or regularly by the sufferer.

Epilepsy

This condition is caused by an upset or disturbance of brain activity and results in a brief dramatic seizure (convulsion or fit). Sometimes casualties have a warning sign (aura) that they are about to have an attack, which can give them the time to get somewhere safe with someone. Warning signs can be a taste, smell or a particular feeling. Some things can cause a casualty to have a seizure, for instance flashing lights, stress or illness.

What will the casualty look like?

At the beginning of the fit the casualty may let out a cry or loud shout and fall or collapse quickly after. Their muscles become rigid and stiff. They may stop breathing briefly, so their colour may be pale or grey/blue around the lips. The casualty may have a red face if they have been holding their breath. Rapid twitching and shaking movements of the whole body may occur. The casualty may salivate and lose bladder or bowel control. The body will then relax after a few moments and the casualty will recover. The casualty may be unsure about what has just happened but may feel extremely tired, confused and upset.

Treatment

If the casualty has had a warning sign, make them safe and comfortable. If not, try to cushion their fall. Allow space for the casualty (maintaining privacy and dignity) to allow the fit to progress. Never try to stop the fit or put anything in the way. After the seizure, put the casualty in the recovery position (see page 75). Check airway, breathing, circulation and allow them to recover.

Complications

Transfer to hospital (999) if:

- the casualty does not recover consciousness
- they have a seizure for more than five minutes
- they have seizures in succession
- it is their first seizure

Mild seizures

Some casualties experience mild epileptic seizures. These are short periods of time where the casualty appears vacant/distant and not aware of where they are. They may stare into the distance, display slight twitching, or make repeated movements such as lips smacking or chewing sounds. This episode may last for seconds or minutes only and can be more common in children. Do not disturb them, but when they have recovered, encourage them to seek medical help.

Diabetes

This condition means that the body cannot use glucose properly because insulin, the hormone which regulates the blood sugar, is low or does not work properly. This means sugar levels in the blood may be high or low and sugar may be detected in the urine.

Types of diabetes

Type 1 – this is when the body cannot produce insulin. It is usually apparent in childhood and is treated with diet and insulin injections. It can also be called Insulin Dependent Diabetes (IDD).

Type 2 – this is when the body does not produce enough insulin or the insulin produced is ineffective. This usually happens in later life and can be controlled by diet. It can also be called Non Insulin Dependent Diabetes (NIDD).

Once someone has been diagnosed with diabetes they may suffer high or low blood sugar levels. Treatments for the two conditions – hypoglycaemia (low) and hyperglycaemia (high) – are very different.

Did you know?

Eating sweets does not cause diabetes. But high-sugar diets over a long period may lead to obesity, which in turn can be associated with type 2 diabetes. With increasing obesity it is predicted that over the next ten years the number of diabetes sufferers in the UK will double. In 2007 there are already 2 million diabetes sufferers in the UK (statistics available from Diabetes UK).

Hypoglycaemia

This is a low blood sugar level and happens very quickly.

What will the casualty look like?

They may have a fast pulse, shallow breathing, and be cold and clammy. They may be hungry, weak and shaking and may be irritable, confused or short-tempered.

Treatment

Calm them down, then give them sweet food or sugary drinks. Allow them to rest and they should recover quickly. If unconscious, transfer them to hospital.

Hyperglycaemia

This is high blood sugar levels and the casualty needs insulin. It is an emergency situation and happens slowly over a few days.

What will the casualty look like?

They may have a fast pulse, slow breathing and a distinct smell of acetone on their breath (similar to nail varnish remover/pear drops sweets).

Treatment

They need insulin, so unless you are medically trained or the casualty can administer it themselves, they need medical treatment, so arrange transfer to hospital.

Complications

If you are dealing with a casualty who is diabetic but you are unsure which condition they are suffering from, do not give them anything until medical help arrives.

Severe allergic reactions

Anaphylactic shock

This condition happens in response to a range of triggers and can be fatal. Examples of triggers include drugs (e.g. antibiotics), insect stings, eating certain foods (e.g. peanuts) and skin contact with chemicals.

In this reaction the body releases chemicals which cause the blood vessels to dilate (get wider) and constrict (make narrow) air passages so the casualty may have low blood pressure and difficulty in breathing.

What will the casualty look like?

This condition can happen seconds after being in contact with the trigger. Breathing will be difficult, so the casualty will be anxious, wheezing and gasping for breath. They may have red, blotchy areas all over their body. They may also have swollen lips and tongue or a swollen area around their eyes. They may be suffering from shock – see shock box (page 65).

Treatment

The only way to treat this condition is with drugs, so an immediate transfer to hospital is necessary. If the casualty carries an Epipen, help them to administer the adrenalin. You should use it only if you have been trained. If the casualty is conscious, sit them up and help them to breathe properly. If the casualty is unconscious, place them in the recovery position (see page 75). Prepare to give CPR.

Complications

If the casualty requires CPR it may be difficult as the mouth and airways are swollen. Always continue until help arrives.

Activity 20

Go to www.bbc.co.uk/health/first_aid_action.
Click onto 'home skills', then caring for adults, then anaphylaxis and complete the interactive test.

Life-saving procedures

The following information complies with the Resuscitation Council guidelines 2005. *Source*: www.redcross.org.uk

Injured person unconscious and breathing – recovery position

If an adult is unconscious but breathing, place them on their side in the recovery position.

1. Place arm nearest you at a right angle, with palm facing up.
2. Move other arm, as shown below, with the back of the hand against the person's cheek. Then get hold of the knee furthest from you and pull up until foot is flat on the floor.
3. Pull the knee towards you, keeping the person's hand pressed against their cheek, and position the leg at a right angle.
4. Make sure the airway remains open by tilting the head back and lifting the chin. Check breathing.
5. Monitor the casualty's condition until help arrives.

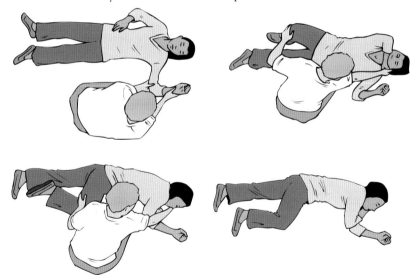

Recovery position

Injured person (adult) unconscious and not breathing

If the person is not breathing normally, you should call an ambulance and then start cardio pulmonary resuscitation (CPR), which is a combination of chest compressions and rescue breaths.

1. Place your hands on the centre of the chest and, with the heel of your hand, press down (4–5cm). After every 30 chest compressions, give 2 rescue breaths.
2. Open the airway – place one hand on the forehead and gently tilt the head back and lift the chin using two fingers. Pinch the person's nose. Place your mouth over their mouth and, by blowing steadily, give two rescue breaths each over one second.

3. Continue with cycles of 30 chest compressions and 2 rescue breaths until emergency help arrives or the person begins to breathe normally.

If you are unable or unwilling to give rescue breaths, just give chest compressions – this is better than doing nothing at all.

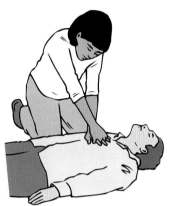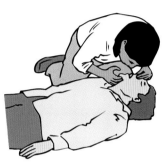

CPR

The Red Cross are the world's leading provider of first aid training. Run throughout the UK, their courses are easy to follow and are presented in a friendly, relaxed atmosphere. To find out more visit redcross.org.uk/firstaid or call 0870 1709222.

Activity 21

With a partner, choose one of the following scenarios. Using role play and first aid equipment, demonstrate your first aid skills to the rest of your group. Make sure you include the following:

● signs and symptoms
● treatment
● complications

Use the following scenarios to practise your skills on the critically injured person for evidence for P3 and M3 in your assignment.

● *Scenario 1*. At work you see a buildings contractor suddenly fall to the ground. There are no signs of breathing or life. You suspect internal bleeding in the abdomen.
● *Scenario 2*. A member of the public visiting your workplace collapses, starts shaking, then appears unconscious. You have checked for signs of breathing and life – both are present.
● *Scenario 3*. Whilst having lunch in the canteen with your colleague, you hear a commotion on another table and see someone coughing, holding their throat and going red in the face.
● *Scenario 4*. A colleague you know is diabetic starts behaving oddly. He shows signs of aggression and is slurring his words.

SUMMARY

- There are many potential hazards within health and social care environments.

- Minimising the risk will reduce the possibility of harm to service users, staff, visitors and property.

- A number of laws exist to promote health, safety and security in the workplace. Enforcing bodies include the local authority and the Health and Safety Executive.

- Each workplace will use the laws in making policies and procedures which employees should follow.

- Employers and employees have responsibilities to promote and maintain a healthy workplace.

- There are many hazards that may occur within local environments. A thorough risk assessment will highlight these and measures in place will reduce the risk.

- Occasionally extra measures will have to be put in place to minimise the risk of harm.

Grading grid

In order to pass this unit, the evidence that the learner presents for assessment needs to demonstrate that they can meet all of the learning outcomes for the unit. The criteria for a pass grade describe the level of achievement required to pass this unit.

GRADING CRITERIA		
TO ACHIEVE A PASS GRADE THE EVIDENCE MUST SHOW THAT THE LEARNER IS ABLE TO:	TO ACHIEVE A MERIT GRADE THE EVIDENCE MUST SHOW THAT, IN ADDITION TO THE PASS CRITERIA, THE LEARNER IS ABLE TO:	TO ACHIEVE A DISTINCTION GRADE THE EVIDENCE MUST SHOW THAT, IN ADDITION TO THE PASS AND MERIT CRITERIA, THE LEARNER IS ABLE TO:
P1 use work placement experiences to explain a minimum of six potential hazards in a health or social care setting		
P2 describe how key legislation in relation to health, safety and security influences health and social care delivery		
P3 using examples from work experience describe how policies and procedures promote health, safety and security in the health and social care workplace	M1 explain how legislation, policies and procedures are used to promote the health, safety and security of individuals in the health and social care workplace	D1 using examples from work experience evaluate the effectiveness of policies and procedures for promoting health, safety and security

GRADING CRITERIA

TO ACHIEVE A PASS GRADE THE EVIDENCE MUST SHOW THAT THE LEARNER IS ABLE TO:	TO ACHIEVE A MERIT GRADE THE EVIDENCE MUST SHOW THAT, IN ADDITION TO THE PASS CRITERIA, THE LEARNER IS ABLE TO:	TO ACHIEVE A DISTINCTION GRADE THE EVIDENCE MUST SHOW THAT, IN ADDITION TO THE PASS AND MERIT CRITERIA, THE LEARNER IS ABLE TO:
P4 examine the roles and responsibilities of key people in the promotion of health, safety and security in a health or social care setting		
P5 carry out a health and safety survey of a local environment used by a specific patient/service user group	M2 assess the risk associated with the use of the chosen local environment and make recommendations for change	D2 justify recommendations made for minimising the risks, as appropriate, for the setting and service user groups.
P6 demonstrate basic first aid skills.	M3 demonstrate first aid skills on a critically injured individual.	

4 Development Through the Life Stages

This unit spans the whole of life from birth to the end of life. It is essential for anyone working with people as it explores the changing needs of individuals as they grow, mature and decline.

Learning Outcomes

On completion of this unit you should be able to:

1 Understand human growth and development through the life stages
2 Understand how life factors and events may influence the development of the individual
3 Understand physical changes and psychological perspectives in relation to ageing

1 Understand human growth and development through the life stages

Activity 1

Linking to P1.

Make a list of people you know who are different ages. Try to choose examples from a wide range of ages. Compare this with a partner.

Do you know someone you think of as really old?

Do you know anyone a lot younger than you?

Compare people from two different age groups. What can they do physically, intellectually, emotionally and socially?

- Physically – can they dress/wash/feed themselves?
- Intellectually – can they communicate with those around them? Are they learning new skills?
- Emotionally – do they express their feelings? Do they understand when others are upset or happy?
- Socially – do they interact with others? Do they have friends?

Life stages

Conception – the beginning of life

Sperm fertilises the ovum and a new life begins. About two weeks after conception the hormone human chorionic gonadotropin (hCG) can be found in the urine and a pregnancy test will be positive.

Pregnancy

Pregnancy lasts for approximately 40 weeks but this varies with individuals. A pregnant woman may feel nauseous, have a metallic taste in the mouth and experience breast tenderness. Physical growth of the embryo is rapid at this stage.

An unborn baby is called an embryo from conception until the end of the eighth week, when it becomes a foetus. Sometimes the embryo does not develop. The pregnancy ends in a miscarriage. Occasionally, a pregnancy is unwanted. The pregnancy may be ended by doctors with a medical or surgical abortion up to 23 weeks 5 days. After that, an abortion is illegal. One of the problems with late abortions is that we now realise that the unborn baby can do more than we previously thought.

Did you know?

Professor Stuart Campbell uses a 4D scanner and has shown that babies start making finger movements at 15 weeks, yawning at 18 weeks and smiling, blinking and crying at 26 weeks. To read more, go to http://news.bbc.co.uk/1/hi/health/3105580.stm.

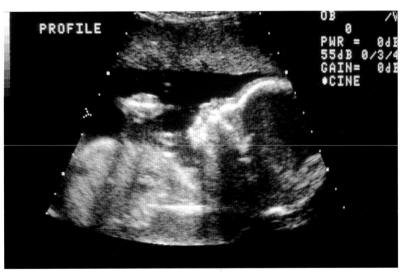

Ultrasound scan of a foetus at 23 weeks

Activity 2

Linking to P1.
Make a list of the reasons why a woman may want to end a pregnancy. Which of these reasons do you think are justified?
Discuss this with a partner. Be sensitive and listen to the views of others.
If you become a nurse, you may be caring for someone with different views to yours. A carer must respect the views of others even if they do not agree with them.

KEY CONCEPTS

Growth is an increase in physical size. Most babies grow bigger.

Development is an increase in skills. Babies learn to talk and to smile. Teenagers learn to use MP3 players. An older person may learn a new language before going on holiday abroad.

Growth is not the same as development. Some people grow but do not develop. Sometimes babies are born with brain damage and do not develop the skills of walking and talking. A pregnant woman who gets German measles may feel unwell. If she is in the early stages of pregnancy, the virus can cause severe damage to the unborn baby. For more on this see www.medinfo.co.uk/conditions/rubella.html.

Birth and infancy

In the last few weeks of pregnancy, the baby settles into the birth position, which is usually head down. Sometimes a baby settles bottom first. This is a breech position.

When the baby is ready to be born, labour starts. The body has been preparing for this event with Braxton-Hicks contractions, where the uterus contracts. Labour is different because the contractions are regular and get stronger. Sometimes there is a show of mucus as the protective mucus plug in the cervix loosens, ready for the baby to be delivered. Sometimes the waters break, leaking fluid from the amniotic sac which holds the baby. The baby can then move further down the birth canal, as the cervix widens. Labour is usually longer in the first pregnancy.

	SCORE OF 0	SCORE OF 1	SCORE OF 2	ACRONYM
Skin colour	blue all over	blue at extremities	normal	Appearance
Heart rate	absent	below 100 beats per minute	above 100 beats per minute	Pulse
Reflex irritability	no response to stimulation	grimace/ feeble cry when stimulated	sneeze/ cough/ pulls away when stimulated	Grimace
Muscle tone	none	some flexion	active movement	Activity
Respiration	absent	weak or irregular	strong	Respiration

Criteria of the Apgar score

Activity 3

Linking to P1.
Watch a video clip of the Moro reflex on http://video.google.com/videoplay? docid=-2508818082092298520&q= moro+reflex

Once the baby is born, the midwife checks the Apgar score at both one and five minutes after birth. The five criteria of the Apgar score are shown on page 82.

From birth to 18 months is a period of rapid physical and emotional development. The newborn baby can see and hear. Reflex actions which occur without thought are already present in a baby's nervous system. They have reflexes such as the startle or Moro reflex. This means they throw out their arms and legs if startled or falling.

Another important reflex is the suckling or rooting reflex. If a baby is touched gently at the side of the mouth it will automatically turn to that side and try to suck. A third reflex is the grasp reflex. If you place your finger in a baby's hand it will grasp your finger.

Some people develop but do not grow because of genetic problems. One example of this is people with achondroplasia. Many people with achondroplasia lead full and active lives. Dr Tom Shakespeare is Director of Outreach for the Policy, Ethics and Life Sciences Research Institute. He is also achondroplasic. According to www.achondroplasia.co.uk, achondroplasia includes short stature. Legs and arms are short compared with the trunk (body); this shortness is more noticeable in the upper arms and legs (proximal).

KEY CONCEPTS

'Developmental norms' means that there are stages of development which people pass through in a certain order. So a baby starts to coo and babble before forming words. Some people think babies should reach developmental milestones at certain ages, or there is something wrong. In fact this is a complex subject. Each child is unique. It is rumoured that Einstein did not talk until he was nearly four years old and some people thought he had learning difficulties. He went on to become one of the most famous mathematicians of all time.

'Psychological' refers to thinking skills. Psychological development means 'developing mentally, learning new ways to think and feel'.

Child of Our Time is a long study over 20 years following a group of children born in 2000. The study examines physical, social and emotional development. It looks at whether the position in the family has an impact on development, what makes children happy and the development of a sense of right and wrong. Log on to the *Child of Our Time* website (www.open2.net/childofourtime/2006/siblings1.html) and read whether brothers and sisters (siblings) matter.

Babies vary in their physical, social and psychological development. By three years old, many variations occur. Some children are talking. Those who hear more than one language may be able to speak more than one language. Children whose parents speak different languages may at times appear to be slow in developing speech, but they are learning two languages at once!

Did you know?

A child who is
isolated from
human company may
not learn to
speak.

Those children who are isolated or hear only baby talk will have a limited vocabulary. Children who are read to regularly will be familiar with books and stories and some can read at this age. Children who hear music and see adults playing instruments may be learning to play a musical instrument.

Children who are used to having people around may be able to cope socially. An only child with limited social contact may be shy. Emotionally, a child who feels secure and loved will gain confidence. A child who has no main carer or who has been moved from foster carer to foster carer may be less secure and less able to relate to others. (See www.bbc.co.uk/parenting/ your_kids/babies_devstagesintro.shtml)

There are many accounts of children living with animals. Some of these are recent. Some are just hearsay, but the following was proved and is one of the earliest.

Case Study
Victor, The Wild Child of Aveyron

Victor was discovered in woods in Saint Sernin sur Rance, southern France at the end of the 18th century. Thought to be about 12 years old, Victor was human in appearance alone. When he was found, he could not speak and behaved like a wild animal. He enjoyed eating rotten food and was unable to distinguish hot from cold. Scientist Dr Jean-Marc-Gaspard Itard dedicated himself to educating the boy, with the aim of teaching him to speak and to show emotion, but Victor's progress was limited. Over the years, the only words Victor learned to speak were 'lait' (milk) and 'Oh Dieu' (my God). His sense of touch was particularly strong and far more valuable to him than his sense of sight. Throughout his life, he was unable to distinguish right from wrong and was indifferent to sex. Victor did make progress, however, in some menial tasks such as setting a table. Victor lived in Paris with Jean-Marc-Gaspard Itard and his housekeeper Madame Guerin until he died, in 1828, aged 40.

To find out more, go to www.feralchildren.com.

Activity 4

Linking to P2.

Talk to the parent of a child under school age. Find out what the child can do and when the child started doing it. Results will vary, depending on the age of the child, their ability and the amount and type of interaction they have with adults.

Remember to change names for confidentiality and be sensitive so the parent is not made anxious.

This checklist may help:

WHAT CAN THE CHILD DO	WHEN DID THEY FIRST LEARN TO DO THIS?
Smile	
Recognise close family members	
Walk	
Run	
Talk	
Use complete sentences	
Stay dry during the day	
Feed themselves from plate when the food is in bite-size pieces	

A child with Down's syndrome

Childhood: 4–9 years

Children develop at different rates from 4–9 years. This is a period of rapid physical growth if the child is well nourished.

There are several possible causes of delayed development. It may be due to genetic disorders such as chromosomal abnormalities. Down's syndrome is one example of this.

Biological issues such as rhesus factor may cause a newborn baby to be jaundiced. If this is not treated, the baby may develop complications such as deafness, blindness, brain damage and learning difficulties.

Environmental factors such as exposure to harmful organisms may damage a baby. The German measles virus may damage an unborn baby, causing deafness and visual impairment. This may delay speech and social interaction as the baby who cannot see does not respond to a smile.

A baby may fail to develop properly in the uterus. Physical problems such as a cleft palate may delay speech.

Socio-economic factors may delay development. Mothers who smoke during pregnancy have lower birth weight babies. According to the National Statistics database, 'women from the manual social classes remain more likely to smoke than those in the non-manual groups. In 2000, 4 per cent of women in the "professional class" reported smoking while pregnant, compared with 26 per cent in the "unskilled" group' (www.statistics.gov.uk/STATBASE/ssdataset.asp?vlnk=5231).

Activity 5

Linking to P2.
In small groups, find out more about Down's syndrome, rhesus factor, German measles, cleft palate and low birth weight. Prepare a presentation for the rest of your class.

2 Understand how life factors and events may influence the development of the individual

The nature–nurture debate

This is a well-discussed topic between theorists and argues whether genetics (nature) or environment (nurture) is responsible for our behaviour and development. Early theorists believed that our personality, intellect, behaviour and gender role were determined by our genes and therefore could not be changed. This meant we would have no free will or control over our actions.

Key principles which are under discussion are as follows.

Biological programming

This area of the debate looks at genetics. Genetics are a blueprint or set of instructions for our development and are unique to each individual. Genes contain the code to guide the construction of our body and are carried on chromosomes which

are arranged in 23 pairs, half from each parent, so we can see parental likeness in ourselves. For example, you may inherit height from one parent and hair colour from the other. The big question is, do we inherit intellect, behaviour or diseases through our genes? This is the nature side of the debate.

Experiences and environment

This side of the debate sees the mind as a 'blank slate' at birth, so behaviour, knowledge and skills are all a result of learning through social experiences. For example, aggression and violence are learned by observation and imitation, so children brought up against a violent and aggressive family background will learn that violence is normal and will have a violent and aggressive temperament. Nurture theorist B.F. Skinner argued that language is learned from others.

Environment versus genetics

As we try to separate the two sides of this long-discussed debate, we realise that a combination of the two sides may be responsible for our development. For example, the genetic disorder PKU (phenylketonuria) is inherited but can be avoided, as diet can help to avoid the serious brain effects associated with it.

Activity 6

Linking to M1 and D1.
Research internet studies looking at identical and non-identical twins and how they have developed, particularly when they have been separated. A famous twin study focused on the Jim Twins, who were separated at birth yet displayed fascinating similarities.

Activity 7

Linking to M1 and D1.
Look at the table below and list people you know who may fit into the categories.

CATEGORY	PEOPLE
Strong personality	
Intelligent	
Aggressive	
Ill health	

Do you think that the above traits are inherited (nature) or socially acquired (nurture)? Discuss your ideas in a group and try to explain your answers.

Activity 8

Reflection for M1/D1.

For merit, your assignment should put forward both sides of the nature-nurture debate, giving examples as to how each can be responsible for development of the individual.

For distinction, your assignment should also include theorists' views, with the advantages and disadvantages of the debate drawn to a conclusion with your views and ideas.

Activity 9

Linking to P3. Look at the development chart for four year olds below.

MOTOR DEVELOPMENT

Sits on chair with knees crossed
Stands, walks and runs on tiptoe
Can bend from the waist keeping legs straight to pick up objects from the floor
Climbs trees and ladders
While running can turn sharp corners
Can walk and run upstairs and downstairs placing one foot on each step
Can kick, catch, throw and bounce a ball
Hops on favoured foot and balances upon it for 3–5 seconds

HAND AND EYE DEVELOPMENT

Names and matches colours
Can pick up crumbs or small objects with one eye covered
Can thread beads but still cannot thread a needle
Builds a ten-cube tower
When shown how, can arrange six cubes into three steps
Copies letters H O T V
Draws a man showing head, legs and maybe arms and legs

HEARING AND VOICE

Talks intelligibly, using correct grammar
Knows and will give own name, age and address in full
Asks what different words mean
Loves hearing and telling long stories
Mixes up fact and fantasy
Counts to 20 and counts actual objects up to 5
Accurately sings and says a few nursery rhymes

PLAY AND SOCIAL DEVELOPMENT

Uses fork and spoon well
Cleans teeth
Washes and dries hands
Will dress and undress himself but needs help with difficult fastenings; enjoys dressing up
Independent (may answer back)
Less tidy than at age 3
Argues with other children but needs their companionship
Learns to take turns and is sympathetic towards siblings and playmates
Understands past, present and future

Activity 9 (continued)

● What reasons can you think of for a four year old not reaching some of these milestones? Hint – think about genetic, biological, environmental, socio-economic and lifestyle factors. Environmental differences could include things such as living in a high-rise flat versus living in a house with a garden. Socio-economic factors could influence how much time adults spend talking or playing with a child. Affluent parents may be able to spend more time with their children.

● Ask permission to observe a three year old. Can the three year old do any of these activities?

Table adapted from www.nuh.nhs.uk/qmc/play/development_charts.htm

Adolescence: 10–18 years

Adolescence is generally marked by the onset of puberty. It is the transition stage between childhood and adulthood. In some Western cultures, adolescence may be marked by emotional turmoil. In other cultures, there is less emotional upheaval.

Puberty is the physical transition from child to adolescent and varies with dietary habits, social and psychological factors. Undernourished children may start puberty later. Better nutrition in the developed countries has been a factor. In 1890 girls generally started their periods at about 15, but now it is around 13. Some even start as young as 8. Boys reach puberty at anything between 9 and 14.

KEY CONCEPTS

Puberty is the first phase of adolescence, the time when sexual maturity becomes evident. A large increase in hormones – oestrogen in girls and testosterone in boys – leads to a range of physical and emotional changes that are completely natural but sometimes hard to deal with.

Source: http://hcd2.bupa.co.uk/fact_sheets/html/puberty.html

Activity 10

Linking to P3 and M2.
You can find out more about the changes that happen in puberty by clicking on the BBC Science website (www.bbc.co.uk/science/humanbody/body/index.shtml?lifecycle) where you can watch an interactive demonstration of the changes that occur in puberty.
If you want to find out more about sexual changes, look at the site www.bbc.co.uk/science/humanbody/body/articles/lifecycle/teenagers/sexual_changes.shtml
Physical maturation may vary with age, culture and nutrition and with what part of the body is maturing. The brain takes longer to mature. We are born with all our brain cells. We cannot grow more if we damage them, but we can develop the nerve pathways between the cells. These are called neural pathways.

Did you know?

Scientists have discovered that the brain's centre of reasoning is among the last areas to mature. The finding, by a team at the US National Institute of Mental Health, may help to explain why teenagers often seem to be so unreasonable.

To read more, go to http://news.bbc.co.uk/1/hi/health/3724615.stm

Adolescence is not clearly defined. Legally in England, the age of consent for sex is 16 years old, but the age for legal drinking is 18 years. In many states in America, you have to be 21 to drink alcohol.

Adulthood: 19–65 years

The age at which one becomes adult varies between countries and has varied in the same country according to the period of history. In Europe in the Middle Ages, people were considered adult at 7 years old. In some Jewish cultures today, people are considered adult at 12 or 13 years old. In Yemen, girls are expected to be adult enough for marriage at 9 years old (source: Human Rights Watch www.hrw.org/wr2k1/mideast/yemen.html). Adults are expected to be responsible, serious, emotionally controlled and able to manage their behaviour.

KEY CONCEPTS

Maturation or maturity is a holistic process. It includes physical, social and emotional aspects. Emotional maturation comes with thinking about experiences. Some young people who have had a lot of responsibility may be very mature in their outlook. Adults are expected to be experienced and wise, but this is not always the case. An older person who has never had any responsibility may lack experience and be immature even though they are physically old.

Ageing is the process of growing older. We are all ageing from the minute we are born!

Adulthood is the age when people usually are economically productive, contributing to the economy by working and earning. Socially, they are able to make their own decisions about when and whether to marry, whether to have children and whether to care for older relatives.

Emotionally, adulthood can be a time to build relationships and also a time to leave relationships.

Activity 11

Linking to M1 and D1.
Think of two adults you know. Are they responsible, serious, emotionally controlled and able to manage their behaviour? Why do you think they meet (or fail to meet) these criteria?

KEY CONCEPTS

A **household** is a person living alone, or a group of people living at the same address who have the address as their only or main residence and either share one main meal a day or share the living accommodation (or both). More people were living alone in 2004 than 40 years previously.

Activity 12

Linking to P3 and M2.
Why do you think the number of people living alone has increased since 1961?

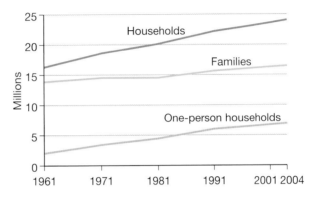

Number of people living alone
Source: National Statistics – www.statistics.gov.uk

Older adulthood: 65+ years

According to the government website, 16 per cent of the UK population are aged 65 or over (source: www.statistics.gov.uk).

Life expectancy

KEY CONCEPTS

Life expectancy means how long a person is expected to live. This varies with individuals.

Life expectancy for both men and women has continued to rise. In 2002, life expectancy at birth for females born in the UK was 81 years, compared with 76 years for males. This contrasts with 49 and 45 years respectively at the turn of the last century, in 1901.

In recent years, the increase in life expectancy among older adults has been dramatic, particularly for men. Between 1981 and 2002, life expectancy at age 50 increased by 4.5 years for men and three years for women. For those aged 65 and over, the extra years of life were three years and two years respectively. By 2002, women who were aged 65 could expect to live to the age of 84, while men could expect to live to the age of 81.

Projections suggest that life expectancies at these older ages will increase by a further three years or so by 2020. The expectation of life for people at 70 and 80 has also gone up. At present there are more older people aged 70 and 80 than ever before.

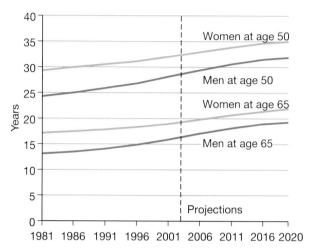

Expected further years of life at ages 50 and 65, UK
Source: National Statistics – www.statistics.gov.uk

Activity 13

Linking to P4 and P5.
Look at the information in the section on 'Life expectancy' on
page 91 and answer the questions:
What has happened to life expectancy – has it got longer or shorter?
In 2002, what was the life expectancy for women?
In 2002, what was the life expectancy for men?
What were these figures in 1901?
Are there more people over 70 now or fewer?

Over the last 30 years death rates for men have fallen faster than those for women, but men still have higher rates than women at all ages. Death rates increase with age, from 8 per 1,000 men aged 50–64 to 188 per 1,000 men aged 85 and over in England and Wales in 2002. The equivalent rates for women were 5 and 160.

Activity 14

Look at causes of death below:

	MEN (%)			WOMEN (%)		
	50–64	65–84	85 AND OVER	50–64	65–84	85 AND OVER
Cancers	39	32	18	53	29	12
Circulatory system	36	42	42	22	40	44
Digestive system	7	4	3	6	5	4
Respiratory system	7	13	19	8	13	17
Injury and poisoning	4	1	2	3	1	2
Nervous system	2	3	3	3	3	3
Mental and behavioural	1	1	3	–	2	6
Other	4	5	9	5	7	14
All deaths (=100%) (thousands)	35.6	144.6	53.6	23.0	129.6	116.3

Cause of death (in percentages), men and women in England and Wales, 2002
Sources: Government Actuary's Department for expectation of life data; Office for National Statistics for mortality data

What is the most common cause of death for those aged 50–64 years?
What is the most common cause of death for those over 65 years?

The most common cause of death for people aged 50–64 was cancers. Overall, 39 per cent of male and 53 per cent of female deaths in this age group were due to cancers. Lung cancer was the most common cause of cancer death for men in this age group. Breast cancer was the most common cause for women. For those over the age of 65, circulatory diseases are the most common cause of death. Within this age group, heart disease as a cause of death decreases with age and strokes increase. Pneumonia as a cause of death also increases with age to account for one in ten deaths among those aged 85 and over.

Note: the expectation of life at a given age is defined as the average number of years which a person could be expected to live if their rate of mortality at each age was that experienced in that calendar year. Projections are 2002 based.

Unless otherwise stated, older people refers to those aged 50 years and over.

The final stages of life

As people get older they may find it difficult to live alone. Their health may deteriorate, eyesight may fail, heart problems may limit what they can do. If they have smoked, they may have lung problems. According to National Statistics Online (www.statistics.gov.uk), 'In 2001, 4.5 per cent of people aged 65 and over were resident in communal establishments in Great Britain. This proportion was greatest among people aged 90 and over.' According to National Statistics Online, 3 in 5 women over 75 live alone.

Activity 15

Linking to P5.
If 4.5 per cent of people aged 65 and over live in residential care, how many do not live in residential care?

Answer: 100% − 4.5% = 95.5 per cent do not live in residential care.

Activity 16

Linking to P4 and P5.
What kind of care do planners need to think about when they see these statistics?
Would they need to provide more home care or more residential care if people wish to stay in their own homes?

KEY CONCEPTS

'**Life course**' refers to the events in a person's life. Sometimes it can be described as a river, starting in the hills as a small stream, running fast, then broadening and slowing as it gets bigger. As it matures and approaches the sea, it slows down. It may be deep and powerful but calm on the surface. Eventually it joins the sea, which is the end of the journey, and for humans, the end of life. Some people have an easy life, with no real problems. Other people have a rough journey, facing obstacles along the way.

UNIT 4 Development Through the Life Stages

Activity 17

Linking to P1.
Draw your own river (see Key Concepts on page 94) and put on the key events in your life so far. Choose things you remember and that have affected you. A young person will be able to draw only the young river because no one knows the future. An older person may be able to draw a longer river and include more events.

Development: holistic development

One theory brings together all the life stages. Erik Erikson (1902–1994) was a German developmental psychologist and psychoanalyst known for his theory on social development of human beings. He developed a theory of eight life stages or crises that we all pass through. He looked at holistic development – seeing the person as a whole, not just a collection of physical systems.

The first stage, trust versus mistrust, occurs when the baby is learning about the world. If the baby is loved and cared for, they may develop a trust that everything will be all right; the world is basically a good place.

The second stage of autonomy versus shame and doubt occurs when the toddler starts to explore the world. If they are supported, praised and encouraged, they will develop confidence. If parents tell them they are bad or naughty, for example if they wet their pants, children may develop a sense of shame and doubt.

The third stage, initiative versus guilt, happens when the child becomes able to explore, play games, be creative. A child playing dressing up may discover the make-up and get creative. If the parent shouts and tells them they are naughty, this may stifle the child's sense of adventure and they may feel guilty about trying anything new.

The fourth stage, industry v inferiority, usually occurs when the child starts school and compares themselves to others. If they are praised for something, they feel happy and work harder. If a child is told they are stupid, they may develop a sense of being inferior to others. This may stay with them for years.

The fifth stage, identity v role confusion, occurs as the child becomes an adolescent. They are no longer a child. Friends may want them to take drugs or alcohol. At this stage, the young person has to decide what their values are and forge their own identity. Sometimes they develop values which conflict with those of their parents. A young person may emerge from this stage with a strong sense of purpose, knowing what is important to them and what they want to do with their life.

The sixth stage, intimacy v isolation, is concerned with relationships. Young people learn to trust others with their emotions and may get hurt. They may decide that they will not get into another relationship and prefer to stay isolated. Many do form intimate relationships, learn how to give and take and learn about commitment.

The seventh stage, generativity v stagnation, is where adults decide to give something back to the community. They have established their family and now develop a sense of social responsibility. One person may volunteer to run a football team for under 11s. Another may become a carer. Those who have not reached this stage may stagnate, feeling they have nothing to offer society.

The eighth and final stage, integrity v despair, is the stage where people look back on their life and either feel content that they have had a good life or are full of regret for opportunities they did not take. You can read more about this on www.business-balls.com/erik_erikson_psychosocial_theory.htm#erikson_psychosocial_theory_summary.

Erikson looked at the continuum of life, where change is social, emotional and intellectual.

3 Understand physical changes and psychological perspectives in relation to ageing

Activity 18

Linking to P5.

Interview an older person about their social network. Remember to maintain confidentiality when presenting your findings. Change names and any details which might identify them. You need to obtain their consent to use the anonymised information. You will have to be sensitive about asking questions. A good way to interview someone is to start with 'Tell me about . . .' Ask open questions such as 'How has that affected you?' This interview schedule may be helpful, or you may prefer to make your own.

● Who is part of their social network? Do they go out to visit friends or do people come to visit them? Do they have a pet to talk to if they live alone?
● Do they live with family or friends, or do they live alone?
● What physical changes have they noticed about getting older?
● How have any of these physical changes affected how they live their lives?
● When do they meet people? Is it every day or not so often?
● How do they keep in touch with people? Do they telephone or email or even write letters?
● Compare your findings with others in your group. Are there any similarities? Are there any differences?

ACTIVITY THEORY	DISENGAGEMENT THEORY
Maintains independence	Encourages dependency
Gives choice	Little choice
Values individuals	Devalues individuality and treats everyone the same

Two theories of ageing

Activity theory

Did you know?

'In its latest projections the Office of National Statistics indicates that nearly a third of the labour force will be over 50 by 2020. Businesses increasingly need to recognise the benefits of age diversity in the workplace.'
(www.dti.gov.uk/files/file29239.pdf)

Havighurst (1963) states that if people keep actively involved with others in a social network, they will be more satisfied with their life. Being an active member of society maintains mental and physical health.

Criticisms of activity theory

Some individuals prefer to live alone and be independent. Not everyone wants to be active. Not everyone is able to participate in a social network. Those with dementia or Alzheimer's disease may have difficulty in maintaining social contacts. People with limited mobility may not be able to go out of the house. Only those able to afford to will participate. Those on limited income may not be able to afford to go out and join activities.

Disengagement theory

In the early 1960s, Cumming and Henry described disengagement theory. They said that social structures encourage older people to withdraw from society so that younger people may take their place. An example is the decline in family size and the break-up of families, which leads to more isolation, especially in older people. They may lose contact with grandchildren after a divorce or separation.

Ageing is seen as a negative withdrawing from society. For many this happens when they stop work. In the 1960s many women did not work. At that time, according to this theory, their role in society finished when their husband died.

Activity 19

Linking to P4, M3 and D2.
Which of the two theories fits your interviewee from Activity 18 best? Are they active or disengaged?

Criticisms of disengagement theory

Society and the nature of work have changed. Many retired older people play an active part in their community and may continue to work in a part time job. Some stores have a good reputation as employers of older people. The old heavy industrial jobs where people, mostly men, were frequently injured no longer exist. Most people work in safe and clean environments, so that when they retire they are not 'worn out'.

The theory denies that individuals have a choice. Not every older person wants to stay at home and watch television.

This theory devalues older people. It does not acknowledge the wisdom some have. A company director who manages a company on Monday, then retires on Tuesday, still has the same skills.

Demographic changes mean that there are fewer young people to take the place of those who retire. If everyone retired early, there would be increased cost to the government for benefits and pensions. People are living longer and staying healthy for longer. Those who retire at 60 may live until they are 80 and are not economically productive.

Since 1 October 2006 it is illegal to discriminate on the grounds of age, so this theory based on age discrimination is technically illegal! Read more on the government website at www.dti.gov.uk/files/file29239. pdf.

Did you
know?

Bingo is good for you!
Older people who go to
bingo keep mentally
active.

Find more theories on ageing on the online website of Geriatric Medicine at www.gerimed.co.uk/sites/Gerimed/downloads/2004aug11.doc.

Read the case study below and decide which theory best applies – is it the activity theory or the disengagement theory?

Case Study

Mary is 82 years old. For the past 20 years, she has made weekly visits to her local bingo hall, where she meets up with friends. As well as the socialising benefits, she enjoys the game because, as she says, it 'keeps her brain ticking over'. Her friend of 50 years, Sue, recently celebrated a £300 win. She claims her success is down to her quick reflexes and the ability to play several bingo cards at once.

The UK Inquiry into Mental Health and Well-Being in Later Life reported in June 2006. You can download the executive summary from www.mhilli.org/documents/InquiryreportPromotingmentalhealthandwell-beinginlaterlife-ExecutiveSummaryandRecommendation.pdf. Its recommendations are shown on the next page.

Activity 20

Linking to P4, M3 and D2.
Which theory is reflected in the recommendations of the UK Inquiry into Mental Health and Well-Being in Later Life – older people should be active *or* older people should disengage?
● Extension activity: which of these recommendations have happened in your local area? Use the government website www.open.gov.uk, then look on your local government website for social services.
What advice can you give an older person to help them become active in society?

WHO	NO.	WHAT
Local authorities	1	Establish 'Healthy Ageing' programme, involving all relevant local authority departments, in partnership with other agencies.
	2	Identify funding for and support community-based projects that involve older people and benefit their mental health and well-being.
Government	3	Introduce a duty on public bodies to promote age equality by 2009.
	4	Ensure that the Commission for Equality and Human Rights tackles age discrimination as an early priority in its work programme.
	5	Ensure that the 2007 Comprehensive Spending Review takes into account the findings of this inquiry, and commit to setting a target date for ending pensioner poverty. Government should publish, by 2009, a timetable for achieving this and report on progress against milestones.
	6	Work to achieve consensus, both within Government and with external stakeholders, on long-term pension arrangements.
Health departments	7	Ensure that active ageing programmes promote mental as well as physical health and well-being in their design, delivery and evaluation.
	8	Ensure that mental health promotion programmes include and provide for older people.
Education departments	9	Ensure that school programmes promote attitudes and behaviour that will lead to good mental health and well-being and healthy ageing.
Public bodies	10	Encourage work practices that support a healthy work-life balance for employees, as a contribution to long-term mental health and well-being.
	11	Abolish mandatory retirement ages and enable flexible retirement for older employees.
	12	Provide pre-retirement information and support for all employees.
Public bodies and businesses	13	Educate and train all staff who have direct contact with the public to value and respect older people.
Age Concern and the Mental Health Foundation	14	Work with other organisations, including the media, to improve public attitudes towards older people and promote a better understanding of mental health issues.
Voluntary organisations and local authorities	15	Encourage and support older people to take advantage of opportunities for meaningful activity, social interaction and physical activity, and provide information, advice and support to enable people to claim the benefits to which they are entitled.

Recommendations of the UK Inquiry into Mental Health and Well-Being in Later Life

Physical changes during the ageing process

The ageing process happens to all adults at varying rates, depending on lifestyle, socio-economic, environmental and genetic factors. Physical changes affect all body systems, but we should remember that the ageing process also brings positive aspects of ageing, for example maturity, wisdom, life experiences and development of self-concept.

Male
- Prostate changes
- Reduced fertility

Both
- May need glasses
- May need hearing aid
- Loss/thinning of hair
- Poor memory
- Slower reactions
- Cardiovascular changes
- Respiratory changes
- Muscular skeletal changes
- Deterioration of sense of smell/taste
- Skin less elastic
- Decline in mobility

Female
- Osteoporosis
- Menopause

Activity 21

Linking to P5.

To investigate the physical changes of the ageing process, interview (with the body systems in mind) an older adult in your work placement or a relative. Get them to discuss their physical changes over their lifetime. Photographs may help to highlight some of the obvious changes.

Remember to talk about the positive aspects of the ageing process. Include this evidence in your assessment for P5 when describing physical changes of the ageing process. The average life expectancy in western society is highlighted in the following link:
http://geography.about.com/library/weekly/aa04200b.htm. Physical changes occur at different rates for different people. These factors may be dependent on diet, exercise, and lifestyle.

Cardiovascular changes

Atherosclerosis

This condition is a build-up of fatty deposits within the walls of the coronary arteries. The fatty deposits are called atheroma, which are made up of cholesterol and waste materials from cells. As the atheroma builds, it forms raised areas in the arteries called plaques. These areas then cause a reduction/slowing of oxygen-rich blood flow to the cardiac muscle and so in turn make the cardiac muscle (heart) less efficient. (For further information about atherosclerosis and its effects, visit www.bhf.org.uk/ publications)

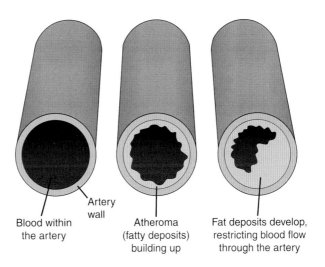

Blood within the artery

Artery wall

Atheroma (fatty deposits) building up

Fat deposits develop, restricting blood flow through the artery

How atheroma builds up in the arteries

Coronary heart disease

All arteries have different names depending on which area of the body they supply. The arteries which supply the heart and cardiac muscle are called coronary arteries, so when they are affected the result is coronary heart disease (CHD).

The heart requires oxygenated blood to function properly and this is supplied via the coronary arteries. If these are restricted by atherosclerosis or blocked by a clot (thrombosis), then angina or heart attack (acute myocardial infarction) can result.

Factors which increase the risk of CHD are high cholesterol, smoking, high blood pressure, physical inactivity, obesity, diabetes or family history.

Respiratory changes

Chronic Obstructive Pulmonary Disease (COPD)

This is a collective respiratory disorder which includes the conditions chronic bronchitis, emphysema and chronic asthma. It affects the respiratory systems, making breathing difficult.

As it is a 'chronic' or long-term disease, it usually affects people over the age of 40. It is responsible for over 30,000 deaths a year in England and Wales.

COPD is usually caused by smoking. Other causes can be occupational exposure to dusts, indoor pollutants, air pollutants or inherited causes, for example some people have an inherited form of emphysema where a lack of protein alpha-1-antitrypsin results in emphysema.

Chronic bronchitis

This refers to inflammation of the bronchi (main airway) to the lungs. The inflammation is due to a long-term infection or long-time exposure to irritants such as smoke or pollutants. The bronchi reacts to these irritants by producing excessive amounts of mucus (sputum), which stops the effective transfer of oxygen through the air sacs (alveoli) to the blood stream.

This condition tends to be worse in the winter when viral or bacterial infections such as colds and flu are more common.

Emphysema

This is also caused by lung damage from infections (chronic), smoke or pollutants and it damages the elastic structure supporting the air sacs (alveoli) in the lungs. Alveoli are grape-like structures where gaseous exchange takes place. This is reduced to a sac structure in emphysema; the result is reduced surface area, therefore reduced carbon dioxide exchange, so breathlessness occurs.

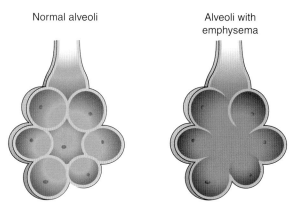

Normal alveoli   Alveoli with emphysema

Alveoli with and without emphysema

Asthma

This is a common respiratory condition often found in children, but if long term (chronic) it can be responsible for COPD, particularly if not controlled. Asthma is an inflammatory disorder which affects the airways. It is triggered by infections, exercise, drug allergies, chemical and smoke fumes, emotions and animal allergies.

In asthma the muscle layer of the bronchi are irritated by the inflammation, which causes the muscle to tighten, thus narrowing the bronchi and resulting in difficulty in breathing, wheezing and coughing.

As asthma is an inflammatory condition it causes mucus to be produced which inhibits the gaseous exchange, making breathing difficult.

Occasionally older adults may be told they have emphysema when in fact they may be suffering from asthma, or it could be genetically linked so therefore an inherited condition.

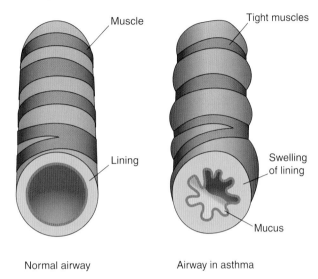

Airway in asthma

Airway in asthma

Skin changes

One of the most obvious signs of ageing are the lines and wrinkles which appear on the skin. Young people's skin is supple and is able to return to its original shape when stretched. However, tissue in the skin loses its elasticity with age, causing the skin to wrinkle rather than bounce back into place.

In a similar way, loss of elasticity in lung tissue means that elderly people are more prone to respiratory problems and diseases like pneumonia. Even eyesight is affected by loss of elasticity – the eye lens becomes less supple with age and is unable to focus as well.

Nervous system changes

Motor Neurone Disease (MND)

This is a rare condition, which is caused by the breakdown of the nerve cells in the brain. Research is under way to understand the causes and develop a cure.

MND usually begins between the ages of 50 and 70 and affects around two people in 100,000 in the UK.

It affects the muscles used to move (voluntary muscles), but not the nerves dealing with sensation, so there is no numbness or pins and needles. The parts of the brain dealing with intelligence and awareness also remain unaffected.

Musculo-skeletal changes

Arthritis

Arthritis simply means painful condition of the joints. There are different types of the disease, many inflammatory and others more degenerative. All age groups can develop arthritis, even children, but usually arthritis occurs three times as often in women as in men.

Rheumatoid arthritis

This is an inflammatory disease, mainly affecting joints and tendons. An inflamed joint looks swollen and red and appears warm to the touch. The disease usually starts in the wrists, hands or feet, and can spread to other joints and parts of the body. Usually, inflammation is the body's way of healing. In rheumatoid arthritis, the immune system starts to attack the body instead of defending it.

Osteoarthritis

This is a degenerative joint disease, which is a gradual breakdown of cartilage in the joints. This chronic condition can cause pain and impair movement, especially in the elderly population. Many people consider OA a natural part of ageing. It usually occurs in the knees, hips, back, hands and feet. It may be limited to one joint, but can affect several joints throughout the body. Around 20 per cent of people over 60 have osteoarthritis.

For further information about physical changes in the ageing process, visit www.nhsdirect.nhs.uk and www.ageconcern.org.uk.

Activity 22

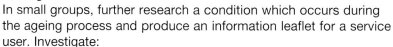

Linking to P5.
In small groups, further research a condition which occurs during the ageing process and produce an information leaflet for a service user. Investigate:

● signs and symptoms
● support available
● treatment
● lifestyle changes/adaptations

Remember

In your assignment for P5 you should describe the physical and psychological changes during the ageing process. You should mention at least one physical change from each system and include both positive and negative aspects of the psychological changes. Refer to your interview with an older service user, which may help you.

SUMMARY

After working through this unit you should be able to:

- describe physical, intellectual, emotional and social development through the life stages

- describe the potential influences of five life factors on the development of individuals

- describe the influences of two predictable and two unpredictable major life events on the development of the individual

- describe two theories of ageing

- describe physical and psychological changes due to the ageing process.

Castle Learning Resource Centre

Grading grid

In order to pass this unit, the evidence that the learner presents for assessment needs to demonstrate that they can meet all of the learning outcomes for the unit. The criteria for a pass grade describe the level of achievement required to pass this unit.

GRADING CRITERIA

TO ACHIEVE A PASS GRADE THE EVIDENCE MUST SHOW THAT THE LEARNER IS ABLE TO:	TO ACHIEVE A MERIT GRADE THE EVIDENCE MUST SHOW THAT, IN ADDITION TO THE PASS CRITERIA, THE LEARNER IS ABLE TO:	TO ACHIEVE A DISTINCTION GRADE THE EVIDENCE MUST SHOW THAT, IN ADDITION TO THE PASS AND MERIT CRITERIA, THE LEARNER IS ABLE TO:
P1 describe physical, intellectual, emotional and social development through the life stages		
P2 describe the potential influences of five life factors on the development of individuals	M1 discuss the nature-nurture debate in relation to individual development	D1 evaluate the nature-nurture debate in relation to development of the individual
P3 describe the influences of two predictable and two unpredictable major life events on the development of the individual	M2 explain how major life events can influence the development of the individual	
P4 describe two theories of ageing	M3 use examples to compare two major theories of ageing.	D2 evaluate the influence of two major theories of ageing on health and social care service provision.

GRADING CRITERIA

TO ACHIEVE A PASS GRADE THE EVIDENCE MUST SHOW THAT THE LEARNER IS ABLE TO:	TO ACHIEVE A MERIT GRADE THE EVIDENCE MUST SHOW THAT, IN ADDITION TO THE PASS CRITERIA, THE LEARNER IS ABLE TO:	TO ACHIEVE A DISTINCTION GRADE THE EVIDENCE MUST SHOW THAT, IN ADDITION TO THE PASS AND MERIT CRITERIA, THE LEARNER IS ABLE TO:
P5 describe physical and psychological changes due to the ageing process.		

5

Fundamentals of Anatomy and Physiology for Health and Social Care

This unit provides an understanding of the anatomy and physiology of human body systems. It begins with cellular structure and function and builds to a more detailed knowledge of the body systems involved in energy metabolism. It provides knowledge of homeostatic mechanisms involved in regulating bodily systems to maintain health. This unit will teach you how to take vital measurements of health and how to recognise variations from the normal.

Anatomy is the structure or make-up of our body and physiology is the function of our body. The human body is made up of various levels of structures. This unit will start with the low-level structure, i.e. cells, then progress towards the complex workings of body systems.

Learning Outcomes
On completion of this unit you should be able to:
1 Understand the organisation of the human body
2 Understand the functioning of the body systems associated with energy metabolism
3 Understand how homeostatic mechanisms operate in the maintenance of an internal environment
4 Be able to interpret data obtained from monitoring routine variations in the functioning of healthy body systems

1 Understand the organisation of the human body

Our bodies are made up of many different types of cells carrying out specialised functions. Examples are shown in the diagram opposite.

Cells

The study of cells is called cytology. All cells develop, change and function together as a specialised tissue. Whatever the specialisation, all cells have the same basic structure and general features. Cells are too small to be seen by the naked eye.

Use Activity 1 to find a description for each of the main components of a typical cell.

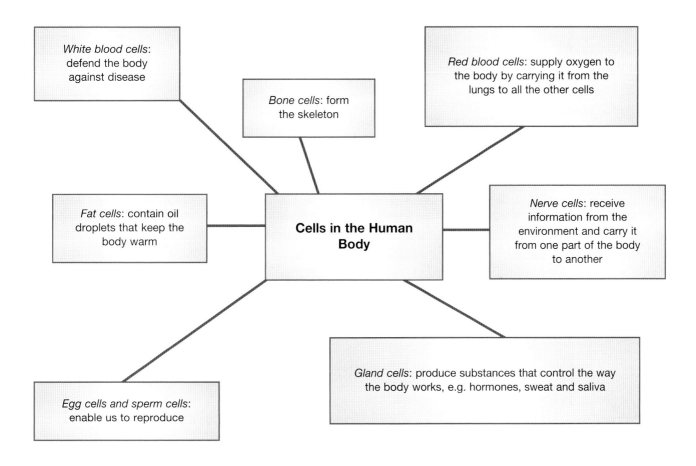

White blood cells: defend the body against disease

Bone cells: form the skeleton

Red blood cells: supply oxygen to the body by carrying it from the lungs to all the other cells

Fat cells: contain oil droplets that keep the body warm

Cells in the Human Body

Nerve cells: receive information from the environment and carry it from one part of the body to another

Gland cells: produce substances that control the way the body works, e.g. hormones, sweat and saliva

Egg cells and sperm cells: enable us to reproduce

Activity 1

This could be used as evidence for P1 in your assignment.
Follow the web link: www.bbc.co.uk/education/asguru/biology.
Click onto cells and then onto animal cells and find out the definitions and functions for the following in an animal cell:

1 cell membrane
2 nucleus
3 cytoplasm
4 organelles
5 mitochondria
6 endoplasmic reticulum (smooth and rough)
7 golgi apparatus
8 lysome

Draw, label and describe the main functions of the above components of a cell.

Cells which function together are called tissues; for example, the cells lining your digestive tract or your respiratory tract are all working together and form tissue.

Tissue types

The study of tissues is called histology. There are four main tissue types found in our body, with special functions. Follow the activity below using the following tissue types:

- *Epithelial*: simple (cuboidal, columnar, squamous, ciliated), compound (simple, keratinised) – epithelial tissue is arranged in a single or multi-layered sheet and usually covers internal and external surfaces of the body.
- *Connective*: blood, cartilage, bone, aerolar, adipose – connective tissue is supporting; it has fibres in it which are tough and non-elastic, e.g. cartilage, tendons, eyeball.
- *Muscle*: striated, non-striated, cardiac. Three main types – voluntary (striated) under control of the brain, e.g. muscles; involuntary (non-striated) under hormone and nervous control, e.g. muscles in the gut; cardiac – found in the heart.
- *Nervous:* consists of neurons to form the nervous system.

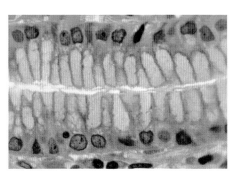

Epithelial tissue

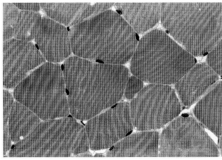

Muscle tissue

Activity 2

This activity will give you evidence so you can complete P2 of your assignment. You need to produce this information individually to formulate a short presentation for your colleagues. You may want to produce handouts.

When listening to your colleagues' presentations you need to take notes and information about websites and books they have used to help you with your assignment work.

Your presentation should include:

- name of tissue type
- an explanation of its structure/inclusion of a picture
- an explanation of where the tissue can be found
- an explanation of the role of the tissue type in the body

Tissues can also be grouped together to form larger structures called organs. So a group of tissues can all work together to carry out a particular function, e.g. the eye, the heart, the liver. Organs have specific functions and distinctive shapes. Activity 3 will help you with P3 of your assignment.

Location of body organs

Many organs in the body function together. This is called a system – for example, the cardiovascular system consists of the heart, blood vessels and blood.

Activity 3

As a class, divide into small groups, each taking one of the following organs:

1 heart
2 lungs
3 brain
4 stomach
5 liver
6 pancreas
7 ovaries/testes
8 duodenum
9 ileum
10 colon
11 kidney
12 bladder
13 uterus

Each group should draw the organ, label it and give a brief description of its function.

On a large piece of paper with a gingerbread person as an outline on it, place your organ and description in its correct location. Display this in your classroom to help you with Unit 5/P3.

The following web link will help with the structure and functions of human body organs: www.bbc.co.uk/science/humanbody. Follow the interactive body link and play the organs game.

Activity 4

Discuss which organs belong to the following systems:

● the digestive system
● the respiratory system
● the reproductive system
● the excretory system

We must remember that some of our body systems are also inter-related, that is to say they cannot function without each other. For example, during exercise, the respiratory system requires more oxygen, so the cardiovascular system works harder to supply this demand. All systems work together to make up an organism, i.e. the living human being. Recap your learning with the next activity.

Activity 5

Fill in the gaps with words from the table to complete the passage about cells, tissues, organs and systems.

specialised	alive	impulses	blood
blood vessels	group	membrane	nerve
muscle	size	structure	shape
nucleus	bone	heart	cells

Cells
There is no such thing as a typical plant or animal cell because they vary a great deal in their _____ and _____ depending on their function.
All cells have a cell _____ which is a thin wall enclosing cytoplasm; this keeps the cell _____. Most cells have a _____; this regulates chemical changes and determines what type of cell it will be.
When the cells have finished dividing and growing they become _____.
This means they do *one* particular job and have a distinctive shape.

Tissues
A tissue such as _____, _____ or _____ is made up of hundreds of cells of a few types. The _____ of each type have similar structure and functions so the tissue then has a particular function, e.g. nerve cells conduct _____.

Organs
Organs consist of several tissues grouped together to make a _____ with a special function, e.g. the stomach is an organ which contains tissues made from epithelial cells, gland cells, muscle cells and nerve cells.

System
A system refers to a _____ of organs whose functions are closely related, e.g. the _____, _____ and _____ make up the circulatory system, while the brain, spinal cord and nerves make up the nervous system.

Answers are provided at the end of this unit.

The cardiovascular system

The heart provides the power to pump the blood around the body through the blood vessels. The blood is the vehicle by which the circulatory system conveys oxygen, nutrients, hormones and other substances to the tissues, carbon dioxide to the lungs and waste products to the kidneys.

The cardiovascular system is responsible for transporting oxygenated blood around the body to the cells and collecting de-oxygenated blood ready for excretion from the cells.

The cardiovascular system consists of:

● the heart
● blood
● blood vessels

The heart

The heart is located between the lungs, slightly to the left in the upper chest (thorax) area. This is the centre of the cardiovascular system and beats more than 100,000 times a day to pump blood through the vessels.

The wall of the heart is divided into:

● the epicardium – external thin layer
● the myocardium – middle layer; specialised cardiac muscle makes the heart contract
● the endocardium – inner layer; covers the valves and tendons

The heart is divided into four chambers and is a double pump. Two upper chambers are called atriums. Two lower chambers are called ventricles. The right and left sides of the heart are separated by the septum, a solid wall which prevents the mix of venous and arterial blood.

The flow of de-oxygenated blood from the right ventricle to the lungs and return of oxygenated blood from the lungs to the left atrium is called pulmonary circulation (it goes to the lungs and back to the heart).

The flow of oxygenated blood from the left ventricle via the aorta to the body and return of de-oxygenated blood to the right atrium is called systemic circulation (it goes to the organs and back to the heart).

How blood flows through the heart

Oxygenated blood from the lungs returns to the heart via the pulmonary vein and enters the left atrium. Blood passes through the bicuspid valve into the left ventricle. From the left ventricle blood is forced out of the aorta (main artery), which carries the oxygenated blood to the rest of the body.

De-oxygenated blood returns from the body to the right atrium via the largest veins of the body, the superior and inferior vena cava. The blood is then squeezed through the tricuspid valve into the right ventricle. Blood is forced through the pulmonary artery, which carries the de-oxygenated blood to the lungs.

Follow the diagram on the next page with the arrows and use these points as instructions to trace the path of oxygenated blood from the lungs, ending with the return of de-oxygenated blood from the body.

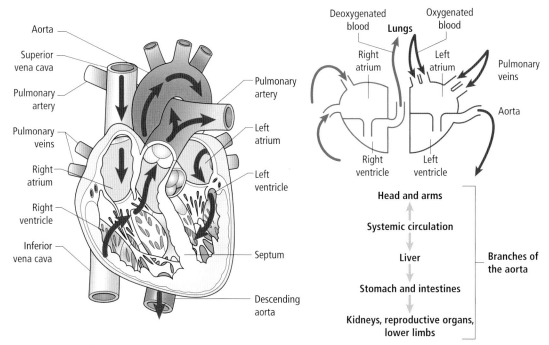

Blood flow through the heart

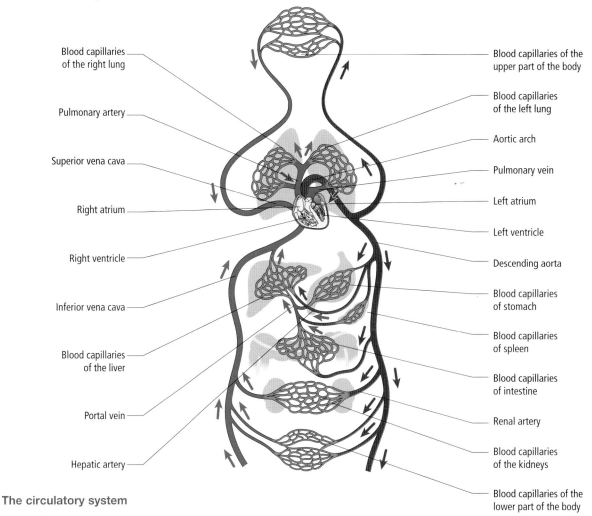

The circulatory system

The circulatory system

The diagram at the bottom of the opposite page illustrates the circulation of oxygenated and de-oxygenated blood.

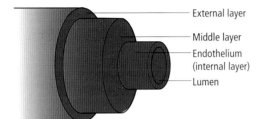

External layer
Middle layer
Endothelium (internal layer)
Lumen

Arteries carry blood away from the heart

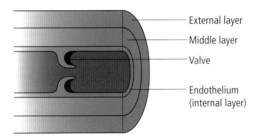

External layer
Middle layer
Valve
Endothelium (internal layer)

Veins carry blood towards the heart

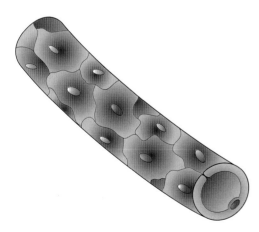

Capillaries are the smallest vessels

Vessels

There are three types of vessels in the body:

- arteries
- veins
- capillaries

Arteries

Arteries have the ability to contract and have to be elastic to expand under the high pressure at which blood is delivered into them from the heart. They then recoil between the beats of the heart. Arteries divide like the branches of a tree to form arterioles and then further divide into capillaries. This allows the high pressure of the blood to decrease and be delivered effectively without damage to organs, tissues and cells.

Veins

In veins the blood is under less pressure so the walls are much thinner. Because the blood travels slower and usually against gravity (uphill), veins contain valves to prevent backflow. A collapsed valve is a varicose vein. Veins like arteries divide into smaller vessels called venules and then into capillaries.

Capillaries

Capillaries are thin-walled vessels which consist of a single layer of cells which are semi-permeable. This allows oxygen, vitamins, minerals and water to be exchanged into the tissues to nourish the cells. Carbon dioxide and water then pass out of the cells to be excreted. This is capillary exchange. Capillaries form a large network of blood vessels all over the body. The more metabolic activity in the tissue or organ, the greater the number of capillaries supplying it (see figure at bottom of opposite page).

Remember

A = Arteries, which carry blood away from the heart.
Which artery and vein does this rule not apply to? Explain your answer.

Differences between arteries and veins

ARTERIES	VEINS
Carry blood away from the heart	Carry blood towards the heart
Carry oxygenated blood	Carry de-oxygenated blood
Blood flows rapidly	Blood flows slowly
Blood flows under high pressure	Blood flows under low pressure
Blood flows in pulses	Blood flows by squeezing action
Walls are thick	Walls are thin
Valves absent	Valves present
Internal diameter small	Internal diameter large
Cross-section round	Cross-section oval

Function of blood

The tables below show what blood is composed of and how the individual components function. Blood as a whole has many important functions:

- transport of nutrients, gases, hormones and antibodies
- defence and protection from disease and infection with clotting factors and antibodies
- temperature control with the homeostatic mechanism for control of body temperature

FORMED ELEMENTS	
ERYTHROCYTES *Red blood cells*	<ul><li>Carry oxygen</li><li>Made in the bone barrow</li><li>Die after 4 months</li></ul>
LEUCOCYTES *White blood cells*	<ul><li>Fight infection</li><li>Made in the bone marrow</li><li>There is one white cell to every 600 red cells</li></ul>
PLATELETS	They help to clot the blood at wounds and so stop the bleeding
LIQUID ELEMENT	
PLASMA	Carries red blood cells/white blood cells/ nutrients/salts

Composition of blood

Oxygen	The blood transports oxygen from the lungs to the cells of the body.
Carbon dioxide	The blood transports carbon dioxide from the cells of the body to the lungs.
Waste products	The blood transports waste products from the cells to the kidneys, lungs and sweat glands.
Digested food	The blood transports nutrients from the digestive organ to the cells.
Hormones	The blood transports hormones from the endocrine glands to the cells.
Heat	The blood helps to regulate body temperature.
Clotting	The blood contains platelets to help to clot the blood wounds.

Functions of blood

The digestive system

The digestive system consists of the mouth, salivary glands, pharynx, oesophagus, stomach, duodenum, ileum, colon, liver and pancreas.

The process of digestion starts at the mouth and completes at the anus. This is the digestive tract or alimentary canal. Digestion is the breakdown of food to enable the body to absorb it into the bloodstream and then into the cells for energy. The breakdown of food is:

● mechanical – by teeth, tongue and gums
● chemical – by digestive enzymes

It is only after chemical breakdown that absorption takes place.

Functions of the digestive system

The functions of the digestive system are:

● ingestion – taking food into the body
● digestion – breaking down the food
● absorption – small molecules are taken into the blood stream
● assimilation – digested foods are used by the body
● egestion – removal of the undigested foods, waste products

Activity 6

Label the diagram of the digestive tract giving a brief overview of the structure and function of each area.

- gall bladder • appendix • bile duct • liver • small intestine • large intestine • oesophagus • mouth • anus • rectum • pancreas • salivary glands • stomach

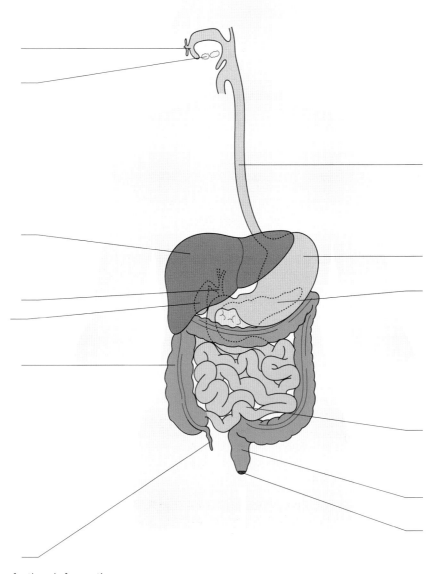

Use this link for further information:
www.kidshealth.org/misc/movie/bodybasics/digestive_system.html

The process of digestion

Mouth

Your food starts its digestive journey in the mouth where mechanical breakdown of the food takes place. The food is chewed and broken into small pieces by the teeth and tongue. This is called mastication (chewing). The saliva causes the food to be mixed into a lump called a bolus.

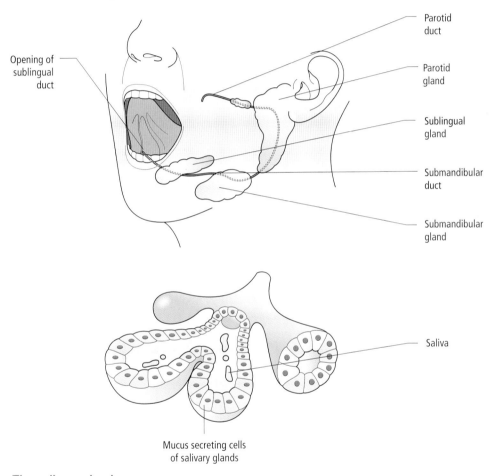

Opening of sublingual duct

Parotid duct

Parotid gland

Sublingual gland

Submandibular duct

Submandibular gland

Saliva

Mucus secreting cells of salivary glands

The salivary glands

The salivary glands secrete enzymes which chemically break down food. The enzyme amylase begins to chemically break down starches (in carbohydrates).

Pharynx

The food then passes through a muscular tube called the pharynx, which leads to the oesophagus. It passes down this tube by swallowing. At the same time muscles in the larynx (see respiration) contract and a flap of skin called the epiglottis snaps shut so that food does not enter the lungs.

Oesophagus

This is a muscular tube leading to the stomach and food moves along by means of peristalsic waves.

Follow this web link to see how peristalsis moves the food down the gut: http://health.howstuffworks.com/adam-200088.htm.

Peristalsis is explained as muscular movement like waves pushing the food. The gut muscles contract behind the bolus and relax in front of the bolus so that the food can move along the gut.

Stomach

The food then passes from the oesophagus through a muscular valve (cardiac valve) into the stomach. The stomach is the widest part of the alimentary canal and food can remain there for up to three hours. The stomach is a J-shaped organ and can be described as a strong muscular sac with many folds inside the lining called rugae. It is here that the food is churned around by large muscles and digestive enzymes are secreted from gastric glands. The food is now in a semi-liquid form called chyme. The enzymes here are called protease (pepsin) and hydrochloric acid. The high acidity level kills most bacteria. The content of the food depends on how long it stays in the stomach:

- fats approximately 6 hours
- protein approximately 4 hours
- carbohydrates approximately 2 hours
- water approximately 15 minutes

Alcohol and drugs are absorbed immediately into the bloodstream from the stomach so their effects are immediate. The chyme then leaves the stomach via the pyloric valve into the small intestine.

Duodenum

This is the first part of the small intestine. It is a long, convoluted tube split into two parts – the jejunum and the ileum. Two large organs help with the digestion of food here, the liver and the pancreas. The liver connects to the duodenum with the bile duct. One of the liver's jobs is to make bile which mainly digests fats. So as food containing fats enters the duodenum, bile is secreted (stored in the gall bladder under the liver) onto the food. This is the first point of fat digestion. Bile salts emulsify the fats – that is, make them into a form where they can be broken down further. They are now tiny fat globules.

The pancreas is a large, slim gland and joins the duodenum via the pancreatic duct. The pancreas pours pancreatic juices via the pancreatic ducts into the duodenum containing the enzymes pancreatic amylase, trypsin and lipase which further break down proteins and fats. The pancreas is also responsible for the control of blood sugar with the hormone insulin (explained in homeostasis, page 126). This hormone is secreted directly into the blood stream, *not* the digestive tract.

As the chyme moves through the small intestine, many molecules are absorbed into the blood stream. The small intestine has a very efficient method to assist this process. It is in the small intestine that most of the absorption takes place. The small

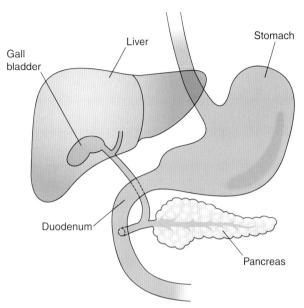

Liver, gall bladder and pancreas

intestine has an excellent blood supply. The inside of the small intestine has finger-like projections called villi, which increase the surface area of the gut. The small intestine then leads to the large intestine through the ileocaecal valve.

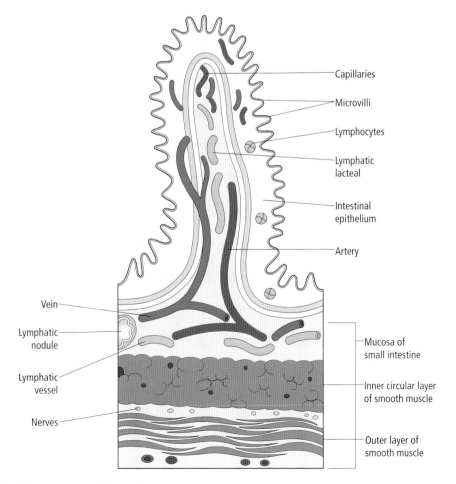

The villi of the small intestine

The large intestine

The large intestine consists of the caecum, ascending colon, transverse colon, descending colon, sigmoid colon, rectum, anal canal and anus. It is wider than the small intestine and is approximately 1.5 metres long. It does not contain villi. The appendix is also contained in the large intestine but has no function in digestion.

The chyme continues into the large intestine and water absorption takes place, plus a little more absorption of nutrients. The large intestine secretes mucus that contains bacteria which ferment any remaining waste products, causing a release of gases. The waste products move through the large intestine (by peristalsis) towards the anal canal where they are expelled through the anus. This is under voluntary control in most adults.

Activity 7

Watch the digestive process following this web link – www.constipationadvice.co.uk/understanding-constipation/ normal-digestive-system.html. Click on the parts of the digestive system to find out more about how they work.

Products of digestion

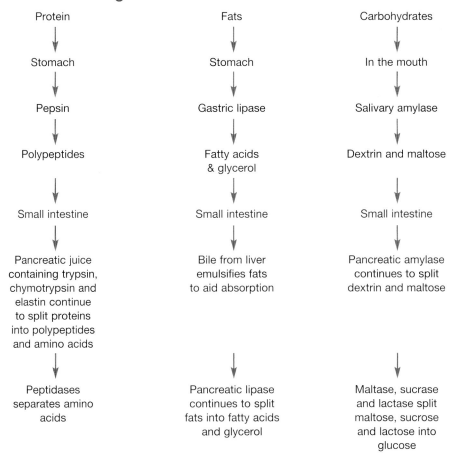

The respiratory system

The respiratory system consists of:

- mouth
- nose
- larynx (voice box)
- trachea
- bronchus ($\times 2$)
- bronchioles
- alveoli

The functions of the respiratory system

- to facilitate inspiration and expiration of air from the atmosphere into the lungs; this is called pulmonary ventilation
- to exchange gases between the lungs and the blood, i.e. oxygen and carbon dioxide; this is called external respiration (breathing)
- to exchange gases between blood and cells; this is called internal respiration (cell respiration or tissue respiration)

External respiration

Let us follow the path of inhaled (breathed-in) air. Air is inhaled through the nose and mouth and flows down the trachea. The trachea is a muscular tube at the top of which is the larynx or voice box. The air is warmed and particles of dust and mucus are trapped by ciliated epithelium which lines the respiratory tract.

The trachea then divides into two, now called a bronchus or bronchi (plural). Then the tubes break into smaller tubes called bronchioles – this is similar to a tree trunk and its smaller branches. It is sometimes called the bronchial tree. At the end of these small tubes are grape-like structures which are one cell thick so as to allow oxygen to diffuse (cross over) into blood vessels which cover the outside of the alveoli. This is where external respiration takes place.

The lungs are different sizes. The left side is smaller to accommodate the heart. Looking at the lungs from the outside, the right side has three lobes and the left has two lobes.

The grape-like structure gives a large surface area to allow maximum exchange of gases. Oxygen diffuses into the blood stream and then goes back to the heart to be circulated around the body. Carbon dioxide is exchanged from the blood circulation back into the alveoli and does a reverse journey through the respiratory system to be exhaled.

In the human lung there are approximately 300 million alveoli – this spaced out would cover a tennis court!

If you look at homeostatic control of breathing rate in this unit you will see that this process is mainly under involuntary control, with our diaphragm and intercostal muscles assisting us with inspiration (breathing in) and expiration (breathing out).

Activity 8

Find out what happens to ciliated epithelium if you smoke. Still fancy a cigarette?

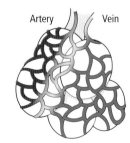

Artery   Vein

Alveoli

Activity 9

Label the diagram below with the correct names listed on page 123. Draw the pathway of inspired and expired air.

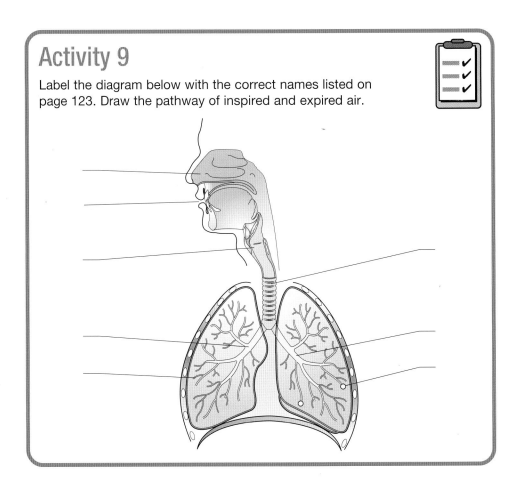

Internal respiration

This can be described as cell respiration. It is the process inside cells when glucose is used to produce energy. This requires oxygen and produces carbon dioxide as a result.

Cell respiration provides cells with energy to perform tasks, e.g. nerve cells are able to send electrical messages (impulses) and muscle cells are able to contract. Therefore this energy is needed for the human being to live.

The energy needed for this type of respiration comes from food, mainly glucose, which is an end product of digestion from carbohydrates. Glucose is taken into the cell and with oxygen a metabolic process takes place whereby energy is released for the body and carbon dioxide and water are left as waste products to be excreted into the blood system and eventually eliminated by the kidneys.

Cell or tissue respiration is different from external respiration. Cell respiration does not mean breathing.

2 Understand the functioning of the body systems associated with energy metabolism

There are many forms of energy, which are highlighted below.

Energy is required in order to perform body functions. Nothing happens without energy. To enable stored energy to work it has to be transferred or changed into a different form. This process requires work and this also involves some wastage.

Energy is never created or destroyed; it is just transferred from one form to another. This is the 'principle of conservation of energy'. For example, a car engine uses chemical energy (the fuel) to make the car move – this is called kinetic energy. So if something takes energy in, it also gives energy out.

The role of energy in our body

Energy is needed for our body to function. It is required for molecules to move in and out of the cells, for breaking down large molecules and also building new molecules. The energy comes from sugars and fats broken down. The cardiovascular, respiratory and digestive systems are all responsible for energy transfer.

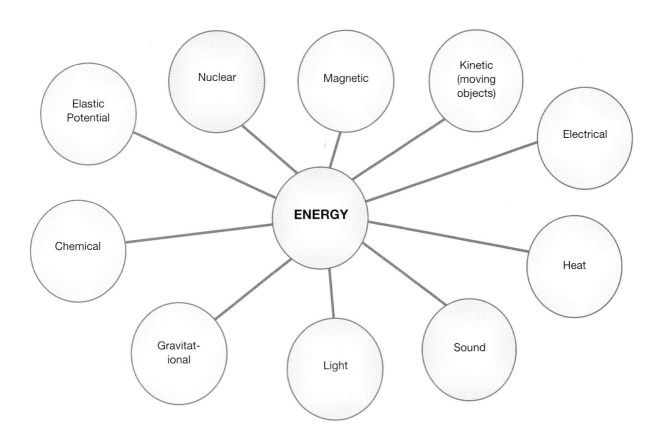

Metabolism

Metabolism is a continual process of chemical changes in cells which allows them to grow and function. It involves constant building of complex molecules (anabolism) and breaking them down (catabolism). These processes often release energy and the speed at which these reactions take place is called the metabolic rate.

3 Understand how homeostatic mechanisms operate in the maintenance of an internal environment

Homeostasis

Homeostasis is the mechanism in our bodies which regulates and maintains a stable and constant environment. The word homeostasis is taken from the Greek meaning *homoios* (same, like) and *stasis* (to stand still).

To help us understand homeostasis, imagine your body is your home and your homeostatic mechanism is your central heating system. Within the system is a thermostat, which regulates the heating system, similar to the hypothalamus in our brain, which regulates our internal environment. This is the control centre.

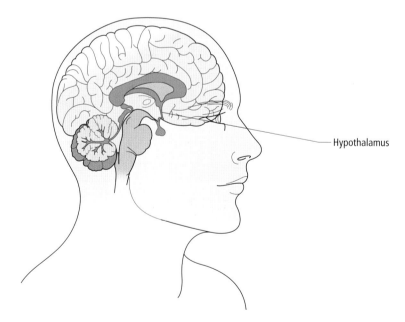

Hypothalamus

Hypothalamus

Our bodies are continuously making adjustments to regulate normal body functions; fortunately these adjustments are done automatically, otherwise we would be very busy people regulating our internal environment frequently. Homeostasis is controlled by the nervous system (autonomic) and the endocrine system (hormones).

Homeostasis is described as a 'negative feedback system'. This simply means that the system is able to take corrective action to maintain a constant environment. This is further explained in the following diagram.

Negative feedback system

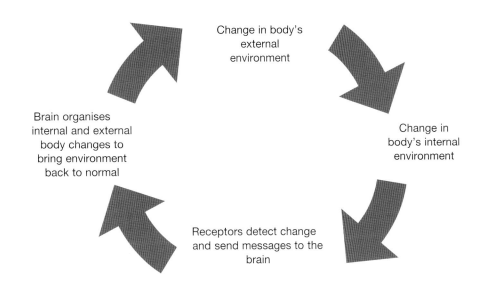

Change in body's external environment

Change in body's internal environment

Receptors detect change and send messages to the brain

Brain organises internal and external body changes to bring environment back to normal

Homeostasis is responsible for maintaining the constant level of many body functions, e.g.:

- body temperature
- water balance
- heart rate
- breathing rate
- blood sugar levels

Activity 10

Visit the following website and discover descriptions and examples for body temperature regulation: www.ergonomics4schools.com

Body temperature

Monitoring of body temperature is called thermoregulation. The adult body's core temperature is held close to 37°c. Temperature detectors in the skin and internal organs monitor this and send messages to the hypothalamus in the brain to take corrective action when it rises or falls.

There are many ways in which we gain and lose heat, e.g.:

- radiation
- convection
- conduction
- evaporation

Homeostasis cannot take place without detectors and correctors. Look at the diagram on the next page and the corrective action the body takes to maintain a constant body temperature.

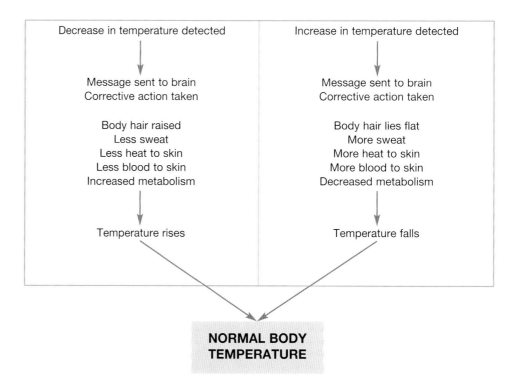

There are also behavioural actions that we take in response to a rise or fall in body temperature, e.g.:

● have warm or cold drinks
● put on or take off clothing
● take exercise
● switch on a fan

Activity 11

In pairs, consider the corrective action the body has taken to get the temperature back to normal and with homeostasis in mind, explain why the corrective action has been taken. You may wish to put it in a table like the examples opposite.

CORRECTIVE ACTION (RAISED TEMPERATURE)	WHY
Sweat is produced	To cool down the body and reduce body temperature
CORRECTIVE ACTION (DECREASE IN TEMPERATURE)	WHY
Shivering	Small muscle movements generate heat to increase body temperature

Facts to consider

Babies lose heat rapidly because they have a large body surface area in relation to the amount of circulating fluid. Their temperature control centre in the brain (hypothalamus) is immature so unable to work efficiently, therefore adults assist in their temperature control with sufficient clothing and bedding. Babies also are unable to shiver and do not have sufficient fat layers to insulate them properly.

Elderly people also find temperature control difficult. This could be due to being less mobile, eating less food and losing nerve sensations so that detectors and receptors work less efficiently.

When the body has an infection, the core temperature can be raised abnormally, thus upsetting the homeostatic control temporarily. In this case the detectors now respond to 37°c being a low temperature, so corrective action such as shivering begins and the body temperature is raised. This condition is known as a rigor.

Breathing rate

Respiration or breathing rate is controlled by nerve impulses from the respiratory centre in the brain (the medulla). It controls:

- the rhythm of breathing
- the depth of breathing
- the rate of breathing

This centre also follows the principle of negative feedback and stimulates a change in respirations when chemo-receptors in the blood sense a decrease or increase in the amount of circulating carbon dioxide. For example, during exercise when the receptors detect a high level of carbon dioxide in the blood stream they send messages to the brain to increase and deepen the breathing rate in order to expel carbon dioxide and replenish oxygen. They do this by sending nerve impulses to the diaphragm (a layer of muscle below the abdominal cavity) which causes them to contract (reduce in size). The diaphragm then flattens and goes lower, thus increasing the space for the lungs to inflate so air is drawn into the lungs (inspiration). The nerve impulses also affect the intercostal muscles (they are between the ribs). These muscles contract and they lift the ribs up and out, again to allow air into the lungs. This is inhalation – breathing in.

Activity 12

For P5.
Investigate the breathing mechanism which is controlled by homeostasis and draw a flow chart to explain what happens during exercise.

Activity 13

Place your hands on your ribs and take a deep breath in. Can you feel your ribs moving up and out? This can also be done automatically during exercise – you don't have to think to breathe faster when running! Explain what is happening to your diaphragm and your ribs.

Did you know?

Breathing rate is also under voluntary control – we can alter our breathing rate or hold our breath if we wish.

Blood sugar levels

The control of blood sugar level in the blood follows the same principle, the negative feedback loop. The control centre here is in the pancreas, where receptors monitor the concentration of glucose in the bloodstream and hormones control the correct balance. The hormones are responsible for the control of:

- insulin – lowers blood sugar levels
- glucagons – raises blood sugar levels

Normal blood sugar level if measured is around 4–8 mmol/l (millimoles per litre). Study the table below to understand the body response:

- after a meal, i.e. high blood sugar level
- when hungry, i.e. low blood sugar level

EATING	HUNGRY
Carbohydrates in food digested and changed to glucose	Low blood sugar level
Glucose high in blood	Pancreas produces the hormone glucagon
Pancreas produces insulin	Changes glycogen from the liver into glucose so it can be used in the body
Some glucose stored in liver as glycogen, some used by cells	Blood glucose level rises to normal
Blood sugar level decreases to normal	Pancreas stops producing glucagon

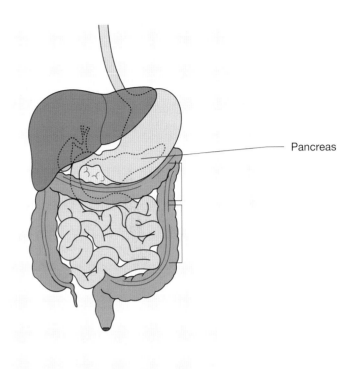

Pancreas

Location of pancreas

Heart rate

The heart rate is under the control of the autonomic nervous system. It is also affected by hormones so is under the control of the endocrine system. The system also follows the principles of the negative feedback system. We do not tell our heart rate to increase or slow down.

What makes our heart rate change?

- exercise
- fear
- excitement

The pacemaker in the heart is situated in the right atrium and is called the sino atrial node; this sends nerve impulses across the heart muscle to other nerves, which in turn stimulate other areas of the heart to beat rhythmically. The other nerve centres are called the atrioventricular node and the Bundle of His.

Go to www.jdaross.cwc.net/cardiac_ cycle.htm and observe the animated picture of how nerve impulses stimulate the heart to beat. This is called the cardiac cycle. The cardiovascular centre in the brain (medulla) modifies the heartbeat according to the messages it is sent via the sympathetic and parasympathetic nervous system. The heart rate usually stays around 70 beats per minute.

If the heart rate needs to speed up, messages are sent along the sympathetic nervous system and the heart rate increases. If the heart rate then needs to slow down, messages are sent along the parasympathetic nervous system and a decrease is made. Detectors which send these messages back and forth are chemical receptors in the heart, blood and brain and constantly measure the acidity of the blood and the level of carbon dioxide and oxygen. Adjustments are made to correct to the normal rate.

The hormone adrenaline is secreted from the adrenal glands on top of the kidneys in times of stress and exercise; this also increases the heart rate and prepares our bodies for actions, i.e. fright, flight, fight.

4 Be able to interpret data obtained from monitoring routine variations in the functioning of healthy body systems

As a professional in a health and social care setting it may be necessary for you to measure and record how the main body systems are functioning. To do this you need to know the following:

- how to measure the system accurately
- what equipment to use and how to use it safely
- what the normal measurements are for that system
- how to record the measurement accurately

Activity 14

In small groups, prepare an information leaflet for a care worker, giving them instructions about how to measure the following:
- pulse rate
- breathing rate
- temperature

Include the following information with diagrams:
- how to position the service user
- how to measure the system
- what the normal range is for an adult
- what equipment you may need

Think about the following:

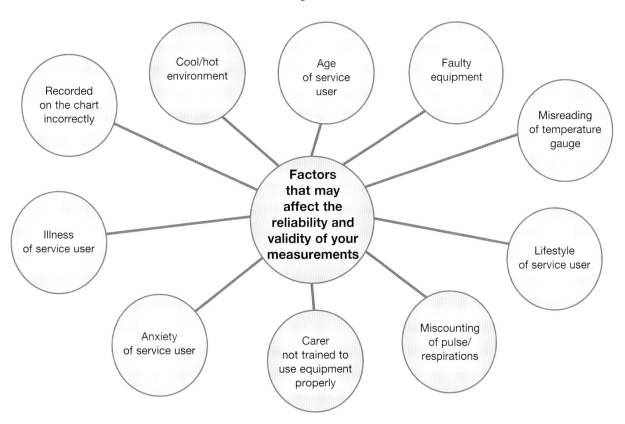

Equipment in care settings should be checked regularly and used according to instructions by people who have been trained.

Activity 15

Can be used as evidence for P6.
In pairs using the Harvard step test (see http://en.wikipedia.org/wiki/Harvard_Step_Test for resources and instructions required), measure heart rate, breathing rate and temperature at the following intervals:

● before exercise
● one minute after exercise
● three minutes after exercise

Record your findings and then comment on what factors may have affected your findings.

SUMMARY

After working through this unit you should be able to:

● describe the functions of the main cell components

● describe the structure of the main tissues of the body and their roles in the functioning of two named body organs

● describe the gross structure and main functions of all major body systems

● describe the role of energy in the body and the physiology of three named body systems in relation to energy metabolism

● describe the concept of homeostasis and the homeostatic mechanisms that regulate heart rate, breathing rate, body temperature and blood glucose levels.

Activity 5 Answer Sheet

Cells
There is no such thing as a typical plant or animal cell because they vary a great deal in their *size* and *shape* depending on their function.
All cells have a cell *membrane* which is a thin wall enclosing cytoplasm; this keeps the cell *alive*. Most cells have a *nucleus*; this regulates chemical changes and determines what type of cell it will be.
When the cells have finished dividing and growing they become *specialised*. This means they do *one* particular job and have a distinctive shape.

Tissues
A tissue such as *bone*, *nerve* or *muscle* is made up of hundreds of cells of a few types. The *cells* of each type have similar structure and functions so the tissue then has a particular function, e.g. nerve cells conduct *impulses*.

Organs
Organs consist of several tissues grouped together to make a *structure* with a special function, e.g. the stomach is an organ which contains tissues made from epithelial cells, gland cells, muscle cells and nerve cells.

System
A system refers to a *group* of organs whose functions are closely related, e.g. the *heart*, *blood vessels* and *blood* make up the circulatory system, while the brain, spinal cord and nerves make up the nervous system.

Grading grid

In order to pass this unit, the evidence that the learner presents for assessment needs to demonstrate that they can meet all of the learning outcomes for the unit. The criteria for a pass grade describe the level of achievement required to pass this unit.

GRADING CRITERIA

TO ACHIEVE A PASS GRADE THE EVIDENCE MUST SHOW THAT THE LEARNER IS ABLE TO:	TO ACHIEVE A MERIT GRADE THE EVIDENCE MUST SHOW THAT, IN ADDITION TO THE PASS CRITERIA, THE LEARNER IS ABLE TO:	TO ACHIEVE A DISTINCTION GRADE THE EVIDENCE MUST SHOW THAT, IN ADDITION TO THE PASS AND MERIT CRITERIA, THE LEARNER IS ABLE TO:
P1 describe the functions of the main cell components		
P2 describe the structure of the main tissues of the body and their role in the functioning of two named body organs		
P3 describe the gross structure and main functions of all major body systems		
P4 describe the role of energy in the body and the physiology of three named body systems in relation to energy metabolism	M1 explain the physiology of three named body systems in relation to energy metabolism	D1 use examples to explain how body systems interrelate with each other

GRADING CRITERIA

TO ACHIEVE A PASS GRADE THE EVIDENCE MUST SHOW THAT THE LEARNER IS ABLE TO:	TO ACHIEVE A MERIT GRADE THE EVIDENCE MUST SHOW THAT, IN ADDITION TO THE PASS CRITERIA, THE LEARNER IS ABLE TO:	TO ACHIEVE A DISTINCTION GRADE THE EVIDENCE MUST SHOW THAT, IN ADDITION TO THE PASS AND MERIT CRITERIA, THE LEARNER IS ABLE TO:
P5 describe the concept of homeostasis and the homeostatic mechanisms that regulate heart rate, breathing rate, body temperature and blood glucose levels	M2 explain the probable homeostatic responses to changes in the internal environment during exercise	D2 explain the importance of homeostasis in maintaining the healthy functioning of the body.
P6 measure body temperature, heart rate and breathing rate before and after a standard period of exercise, interpret the data and comment on its validity.	M3 analyse data obtained to show how homeostatic mechanisms control the internal environment during exercise.	

Personal and Professional Development in Health and Social Care

This is a double unit which brings together learning from other parts of the course. The focus of this unit is on developing yourself as a person and developing your professional practice. This is the most important unit of the course because it is where you learn what it means to be professional. A minimum of 100 hours of work experience divided between at least three different placements is required for this unit.

Learning Outcomes

On completion of this unit you should be able to:

1 Understand the learning process
2 Plan for, monitor and reflect on your own development
3 Understand service provision in the health or social care sectors

1 Understand the learning process

Theories of learning

In order to survive we have to learn. A newborn baby quickly learns how to breathe, cry and suck. Soon the baby learns to recognise the mother's face. A lot of learning happens before the child goes to school.

Theories of learning attempt to explain what happens when we learn. There are many theories of how we learn. In this section we examine Kolb's theory and a later theory developed by Honey and Mumford. These are important theories used by those involved in education, but there are many more. If you are interested in the learning process you can find out more on websites such as:

- www.funderstanding.com/about_learning.cfm
- www.psychology.org

KEY CONCEPTS

Experiential learning refers to learning by experience. This is different to learning from a book.

Kolb's experiential learning theory

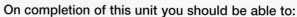

David Kolb's theory builds on three major theories of learning, those of Jung, Piaget and Rogers.

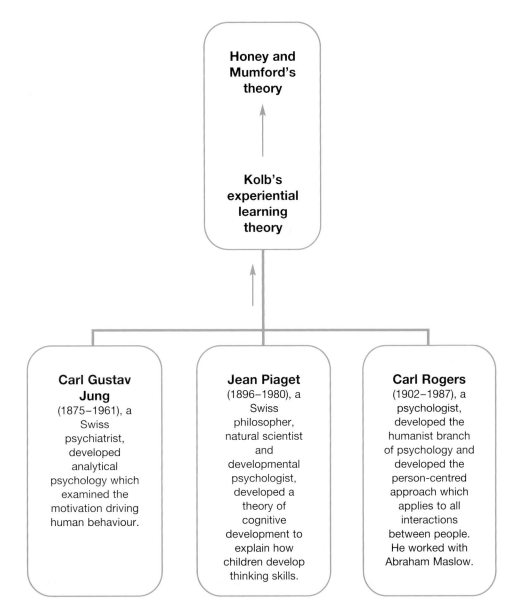

Kolb's theory focuses on learning by experience. He suggests we learn in the following stages:

- concrete experience (CE) – this means we experience an event such as getting sun burn
- reflective observation (RO) – we then reflect on the experience and consider why we got burned
- abstract conceptualisation (AC) – as a result of reflecting we might develop the general idea that going in the sun without sun block is a bad idea
- active experimentation (AE) – next time we go in the sun we use sun block to see whether that prevents sunburn

Kolb suggests this is a spiral, so that when we have completed stage 4 we apply that to a new concrete experience. Thus when we go on holiday to a hot country we may take sun block and a hat. We can apply this learning spiral to anything.

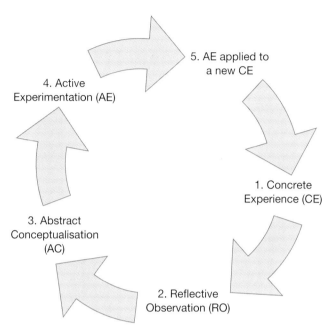

Kolb's learning spiral

Think of your work placement. Perhaps on your first day you had difficulty remembering people's names. You reflect on this and find a way of remembering, then apply it next time you go to placement. When you next go to a new placement, your memory of how you learned people's names last time will help you learn names quicker this time.

Activity 1

Helping towards P5.
Think of an event or incident that happened to you at placement.
● Describe the situation. This is concrete experience.
● Think about the situation. Why did it happen? What happened? Could it have worked out differently if you had reacted differently? This is reflective observation.
● What have you learned about this type of situation? This is abstract conceptualisation.
● Next time you meet a similar situation, what will you do differently? This is active experimentation.

KEY CONCEPTS

Learning styles are the preferred way or ways that people learn.

Remember

The learning spiral describes preferred learning styles, but some people use more than one learning style.

Kolb's learning styles

Kolb used the idea of a learning spiral to develop a theory of learning styles. He suggested that:

● CE is involved with feeling
● AE is involved with doing
● AC is involved with thinking
● RO is involved with watching

People are usually either watchers or doers. They either think logically or feel intuitively.

The following grid shows Kolb's four learning styles.

	DOING (AE)	WATCHING (RO)
FEELING (CE)	accommodating (CE/AE)	diverging (CE/RO)
THINKING (AC)	converging (AC/AE)	assimilating (AC/RO)

You can often tell a person's preferred learning style by watching how they deal with a situation. Assembling flat-pack furniture can be extremely stressful for some couples because they have different learning styles.

A diverging learner prefers to watch rather than do. They learn by feeling then reflecting using a diverging learning style (CE/RO). They would get a 'gut feel' or 'intuition' for putting together a flat-pack wardrobe, take a long time to get started, then reflect why it did or didn't work.

The assimilating learner prefers a concise, logical approach. They are thinkers rather than doers. They use the assimilating learning style (AC/RO). An assimilating learner would logically work out what the finished wardrobe should look like and think where each piece should go and what might happen if a piece went in the wrong way. They may spend time watching others before doing anything themselves.

Convergent thinkers are 'doers'. They use abstract conceptualisation and active experimentation (AC/AE). A convergent thinker might think what the wardrobe should look like, then try placing a few pieces together, moving them round until they fit.

Those with accommodating learning style are 'hands on' and use 'gut instinct'. They use concrete experience and active experimentation (CE/AE). They might get a feel for it, put pieces together, then have to take them apart when they don't fit.

Activity 2

Help with P5.
Think about it. Instead of a flat-pack wardrobe, imagine your portfolio for Unit 6. What kind of learner are you? Do you:

- take a long time to get started, then throw everything in and wonder why your tutor says it has not met the criteria? CE/RO
- think about what type of evidence is needed and where it should go in your portfolio, but spend so much time thinking about it you don't get started? AC/RO
- think about what you need and try putting a few pieces of evidence together? AC/AE
- start collecting evidence and put it in your folder, but be prepared to move it to another section? CE/AE

If you recognise your preferred learning style and it is not very effective, you may wish to practise a different style when assembling your portfolio!

Learning styles – Honey and Mumford

Peter Honey and Alan Mumford worked in the 1970s and developed Kolb's model further. They used four learning styles:

- activists – people who prefer to act rather than think
- reflectors – those who prefer to stand back and gather evidence
- theorists – people who like to think things through logically
- pragmatists – people who are practical – they prefer to get on with a job and can make decisions quickly

> You are born with all your potential.

> Your family helps you develop social skills and shapes your first attitudes to learning. A hardworking parent may inspire the child to work hard too. Parents who read to their children show them that reading is important.

> School further influences your attitudes to learning. If you are praised, you do well. If you are criticised, you become demotivated.

Activity 3

Linking to P1, M1, D1.
In pairs or groups of three, research different learning styles from the following:
- Kolb
- Honey and Mumford
- Gardner's Multiple Intelligences and VAK learning styles models
- Benziger's Thinking Styles and Brain Dominance
- Bloom's Taxonomy of Learning Domains.

Prepare a presentation for your group. One person should prepare a PowerPoint presentation, one person should summarise the information in a poster and one person should prepare a leaflet to explain the learning style to a 16-year-old college student.
A good source for this is www.businessballs.com.

Influences on learning

Whether you are a 'good learner' or a 'poor learner' is influenced by many factors. You may be a poor learner when it comes to riding a bike, but a good learner when remembering the words of a new song. In this section, we will explore some of the influences on learning. You will also learn how to improve your learning technique.

We are all different. Some people are naturally good at reading and writing. Some people have to work hard to learn how to spell, and struggle to write assignments. What makes us different? Why are some people better at some things than others?

We are all born with potential skills and abilities. How we develop varies with our physical, social and emotional environment. The flow chart opposite explains how some factors can influence our learning.

Activity 4

Linking to P1 and P2.
Your past, present and future all influence your learning. Copy and complete this table:

My previous experience of learning has been enjoyable/ difficult because	At present I am enjoying /not enjoying learning because	In the future I want to ....
		The problems I will face are ....
Key influences in my previous learning have been	What I can do to improve my learning is	I will/will not be able to overcome these problems because ....

Sometimes people have specific learning needs.

● A speaks Urdu as her first language and English only when outside the home. Her written English is weak, but her spoken English is not a problem.
● B gets his letters mixed up when reading and writing. He often mixes up 'b' and 'd'. At school he was told he could not spell but he was not taught how to improve.

The college offers assessment and support for students with dyslexia. It also offers English courses for speakers of other languages. Which support do you think would help A?

A would benefit from attending classes for English for speakers of other languages. B would benefit from having an assessment and then having specialist support if he has dyslexia.

Did you know?

One in ten people have dyslexia. Many people with dyslexia are of above-average intelligence. Famous people with dyslexia include Richard Branson and Bill Gates.

You can get help and advice from the British Dyslexia Association website: http://www.bdadyslexia.org.uk /helpline.html

Which is better – formal learning or informal learning?

We never stop learning. From before we are born until we die, our brains are working. Have you ever been stuck with a problem, given up and gone to bed? Next morning the solution may just come to you. This is because our brain is programmed to think even when we are not consciously working on a problem.

Babies learn to speak their first language and to walk without any formal learning. No one ever sits a baby at a desk and instructs them in English grammar, yet by the time they are four or five they have worked it out for themselves. Ten years later, that same person struggles to learn a foreign language at school using formal learning

Did you know?

Jamie Oliver learned to cook as a youngster in his mum and dad's pub restaurant.

At the age of thirteen, Noel Gallagher received six months' probation for robbing a corner shop. While on probation, he taught himself to play guitar.

methods. Babies learn informally. Children learn to ride a bike or kick a ball by watching others and practising. A baby learning to walk may drop onto his bottom several times, but each time he gets up and tries again. This way he learns to walk.

As we get older we sometimes forget this way of learning. When we make a mistake or fail at the first attempt, we may give up and never learn a particular skill. Some people think they are no good at reading or writing because they made a few mistakes at first. Remember – a person who never made a mistake never made anything! Some people learn better through informal learning. Formal learning is useful when you need to gain a qualification, but most of our learning is informal.

Some factors which influence learning are shown in the table below.

Activity 5

Linking to P3, P4, M2 and D2.
Which of the factors in the table below apply to you? If you ticked factors in the column 'Things which can stop you learning', make a plan for how you can change these factors.

THINGS WHICH HELP YOU LEARN	THINGS WHICH CAN STOP YOU LEARNING
Good time management Your aspirations and motivation A positive attitude Being self-disciplined Having reasonable health Being in a secure and supportive relationship Prioritising what is important and what is urgent Sharing your knowledge with others Having resources such as a computer and a printer and knowing how to use them effectively Know your learning style and how you learn best	Wasting time Not knowing what you want to do with your life Being negative Giving up after a setback Having too many responsibilities, for example having three jobs, a family and trying to study Being in a relationship where your partner does not value what you are doing Being indecisive – not knowing what is important to you Having resources which you do not know how to use Not knowing your own learning style Not knowing how to study effectively

Factors that influence learning

Skills for learning

Studying is a skill, just like riding a bike or swimming – anyone can learn these skills. But just like riding a bike, you need to practise to get good at it. There are lots of tips to help you improve your study technique.

Think about:

- how you study
- when you study
- where you study

In Activity 6, you will find a tip about how to study.

Activity 6

Linking to P3.
When you need to read a chapter or an article, follow this process, known as the **SQ3R method**.

- Survey the material. Flick through just as you would with a magazine.
- Question – are there any pictures or cartoons? Does the material look interesting or boring? What do you know of the subject already? Do you really need to read the chapter? If you do need to read the chapter, move on to the 3R stage.
- Read the material with a pencil in your hand. If it is your own copy of the book or your own photocopy of the material, mark in the margin. Establish a code. You might have a star for an interesting example, or a question mark for something you do not understand.
- Now close the book. Recall the material. Take a clean piece of paper and jot down anything you can remember about what you read. Use pictures if it helps. You will not remember everything, but you may remember something.
- Open the book. Review the material. Use a different coloured pen, open the book and add any notes you missed.

You will need to do this a few times before you feel comfortable with the method.

When do you study?

When do you feel most awake, at night or in the morning? If you can leap out of bed at 6am, alert and ready to study, use that time. Many people study in the evening, but that is not always the best time. Your brain may be tired and you may not be able to remember what you study if you are tired.

How long do you study for, one hour or two hours? In fact, our brains get tired after about 20 minutes and we need to vary the activity. If you have an hour to study, plan a variety of activities.

In 60 minutes you can:

- sort your notes – 5 minutes
- use the SQ3R method to make notes – 20 minutes
- word process a draft assignment – 20 minutes
- write up your placement diary – 10 minutes
- and still have time for a cup of coffee – 5 minutes!

Did you know?

If you spend ten minutes every day looking for pen and paper, you could waste over an hour a week.

Where do you study?

Do you waste time looking for your notepad, pen and textbook? Or do you have a place where you can leave your books ready to start work as soon as you have time?

Literacy, numeracy and information technology

Most students have at some time studied literacy, numeracy and IT, but these topics are essential in health and social care.

Literacy matters because written communication is an important way for professionals to share information. Just imagine what could happen if a doctor or nurse could not spell and guessed at a person's medication. The patient might get the wrong drug!

Information technology is important for email communication and for storing information. The government plans to have all patient records held on computer in the near future. General practitioners already keep patient information on computer. Computer skills are essential in health and social care.

The spelling and grammar checker helps students, but proof-reading is essential. Read this poem and spot the mistakes:

I halve a spelling chequer
It came with my pea sea
It plane lee marques four my revue
Miss steaks aye ken knot sea

Numeracy matters because the ability to use numbers in a practical situation is vital in care work. Morphine is a strong drug used to relieve pain. The usual dose for an intramuscular injection is 10 mg. 100 mg may kill you. Would you like to have an injection from a nurse who could not tell the difference between 10 mg and 100 mg?

Did you know?

If you are worried about your literacy, numeracy or computer skills, you can brush up online with games and quizzes at:

http://www.bbc.co.uk/keyskills
http://www.bbc.co.uk/skillswise
http://www.bbc.co.uk/raw

Did you know?

A nurse, midwife or specialist community public health nurse must work to the NMC code of professional conduct: standards for conduct, performance and ethics.

Research skills

Anyone hoping to work in a health and social care profession must have a good understanding of research because practice is 'evidence based'. This means what you do as a professional is based on research findings. You cannot say that you followed a procedure because someone told you to do it. Professionals are accountable for their own practice. This means they may have to justify what they do before a panel of other professionals.

As a registered nurse, midwife or specialist community public health nurse, you are personally accountable for your practice. In caring for patients and service users, you must:

- respect the patient or service user as an individual
- obtain consent before you give any treatment or care
- protect confidential information
- cooperate with others in the team
- maintain your professional knowledge and competence
- be trustworthy
- act to identify and minimise risk to patients and service users

These are the shared values of all the United Kingdom health care regulatory bodies. This updated version of the code was published in November 2004 (source: http://www.nmc-uk.org).

Research should be objective, valid and reliable. It is not based on opinions but as far as possible on what has been observed or discovered through interview or questionnaire, using unbiased questions. Research is accepted only when it has been reviewed by other expert professionals. As a student you will practise the methods used for research, just as a trainee pilot practises in a flight simulator. Perhaps one day you too may conduct groundbreaking research as part of a PhD!

Reflection and using feedback

A professional worker in health or social care is expected to reflect on their practice and improve. One way to improve what you do is to listen for feedback.

Donald Alan Schön wrote *The Reflective Practitioner* (Schön, 1983) in which he suggested that there are two types of reflection. There is reflection in action, when a person is in the situation and thinks how they can improve that situation. There is also reflection on action, after the event, when a person thinks back and says, 'If that happened again I would do that differently'. Both types of reflection are essential for professionals. (See 'Reflecting on your own development' on page 167.)

Activity 7

Towards P7.

Case Study

Jane, a staff nurse, was on duty in casualty one busy Saturday night. Mrs B was admitted but could not be seen for four hours because the doctor was busy with people who had been injured in a road traffic accident. Jane took time out to explain to Mrs B that the doctor would see her as soon as he could. She made Mrs B comfortable on the trolley and gave her an extra blanket. The doctor prescribed something for the pain. Mrs B thanked Jane.

Jane reflected on the situation and felt that she had done a good job that night. Even though she could not do any more for Mrs B, she had kept her informed of what was happening.

Contrast Jane's shift with Kylie's shift the next day. Casualty was rather quiet. Miss C came in with severe pain in her eye. The eye was swollen, watering and very red. Miss C was in a lot of pain. The receptionist told her to sit and wait her turn. Kylie, a

Activity 7 (continued)

staff nurse, was standing at the nurse station, talking to her friend about their night out the previous evening. Neither of them spoke to Miss C. Another woman arrived at casualty. She had been seen the previous day and had come for a check-up. She was laughing and chatting with her family and did not seem to be in any discomfort.

Two hours later, Miss C had not been seen. No one told her what was happening. Several people came, were seen by the doctors and left. Kylie and the receptionist were now browsing through the magazines in the waiting room and had not spoken to Miss C. After another hour, Miss C made an official complaint about Kylie.

What do you think Kylie could have done differently?

Support for learners

What do we mean by support? There is a Chinese saying: 'Give a man a fish and you feed him for a day. Teach a man to fish and you feed him for a lifetime.'

Support is not doing the work for you, support is teaching you how to do the work. So who can help when you are stuck and don't understand the work?

I'm sure you know the tutors who will take time to explain. Friends can also help. Sometimes a whole group finds a topic difficult. By talking to others in your group, your peers, you may find that no one understands a topic such as referencing. If this is the case, your tutor will need to go over the topic again so you all understand.

Placement is a good source of help. Supervisors and mentors are there to help. Supervisors will explain if you do not understand what you have to do. Mentors offer a friendly ear and can often suggest ideas for tackling a subject. Remember – no one can do the work for you.

Sometimes a formal meeting may provide information, for example a case conference about a service user may help you to understand the background of the person you are caring for.

One of the best ways to learn is to develop self-awareness.

Case Study

Jenny was shy and found it difficult to talk to people. At placement she got on with the jobs but never spent time talking to service users or relatives. Jenny was horrified one day to be told that the service users and their visitors considered her to be stuck-up. As she thought about it, Jenny could see why they thought that. Whenever a relative arrived, she went to make a cup of tea for them, but never said 'Hello'. As Jenny developed self-awareness, she realised that she had to put herself in the other person's place. How would she feel if she arrived at a care home and the carer walked off without saying a word? Gradually, Jenny overcame her shyness and a year later she was voted friendliest carer by all the staff, residents and relatives!

Jenny developed self-awareness and as a result improved her practice. Sadly, not everyone is willing to listen to feedback. Some people say, 'I've done this job for years – you can't teach me anything!' When you hear this, you know the person has little self-awareness. Only a person with a closed mind thinks they know it all. Not surprisingly, they never improve their practice. As the NLP saying goes: 'If you always do what you've always done, you'll always get what you've always got.'

Keep your ears open and make a note when you hear someone saying they know it all. You can even learn something from them – you can learn what type of thinking to avoid. Don't get stuck like they have!

How and where to access information and support on knowledge and best practice

Professionals need to keep up to date. The Nursing and Midwifery Council Code of Conduct states that the nurse, midwife or specialist community public health nurse must maintain 'professional knowledge and competence' (www.nmc-uk.org).

The General Social Care Council Code of Conduct 2002 for Employers of Social Care Workers states that 'only people who have the appropriate knowledge and skills' may enter the workforce. The code of conduct for Social Care Workers states they must 'be accountable for the quality of their work and take responsibility for maintaining and improving their knowledge and skills' (www.gscc.org.uk/Home).

Many professionals read journals regularly in order to keep up to date. Social workers may read *Community Care*, while nurses may read *Nursing Standard*, the journal of the Royal College of Nursing, or *Nursing Times*.

Increasingly, professionals need to use online journals and websites as change is rapid in this sector.

Activity 8

Linking to P5.

Make a list of useful websites and keep it in your portfolio.
Here are a few to start you off, but you will need to add to them.

WEBSITE	USEFUL FOR
www.gscc.org.uk	Information for social care and for codes of conduct
www.nmc-uk.org	Information for nursing, midwifery and specialist community public health nurses and for code of conduct
www.rcn.org.uk	The Royal College of Nursing website has information on health policy from a nursing point of view
http://direct.gov.uk	The official government website has links to legislation, policies and other government websites
www.nhs.uk	Find out how the NHS works, its history and current developments in the NHS
www.dh.gov.uk	Anything to do with health policy, statistics and hospital performance
www.cjsonline.gov.uk	The gateway page for anything to do with criminal justice in England and Wales

There are lots more.
- See how many relevant websites you can find
- You may want to have a list for each unit
- Look at the voluntary sector too for useful websites

Learning opportunities

Formal v informal

Activity 9

Linking to P1, M1, D1.
Make a table like the one below for yourself. List the things you learned informally before starting school. (You may have to ask a parent or an older brother or sister if you cannot remember.)
Now make a list of the things you learned formally in class.
Continue each list, adding the informal learning you acquired from friends as a teenager.
Look forward and have a guess whether your future learning is likely to be mostly formal or informal.
What conclusions can you draw about the importance of formal versus informal learning?

	INFORMAL LEARNING	FORMAL LEARNING
Before starting school		
From 5–11 years		
From 12–19 years		
From 20–59 years		
60 years and above		

From Activity 9 you can see that learning opportunities occur everywhere. Important skills such as time management, problem solving, taking responsibility and communicating effectively can be learned just as well outside the classroom.

Activity 10

Linking to P3.
Use the following headings and list three things you can learn from each situation that will help you develop as a person and as a professional worker in health and social care.

PLACEMENT	INDEPENDENT STUDIES	LIFE EXPERIENCE	EMPLOYMENT	VOLUNTARY ACTIVITIES

2 Plan for, monitor and reflect on your own development

At the start of the course you may have had some knowledge of health and social care. You may have had some of the skills needed in this area and you may have decided on a career. By the end of the course you may still want the same career, or you might have changed your mind as you discover more about this area. An occupational therapist at placement might inspire you to think of occupational therapy as a career. Speaking to a mental health nurse might help you to consider that as a possible avenue. Part of learning is that you can change your mind.

Whether you decide to become a nurse, a social worker or opt for any of the other careers in this field, self-awareness and self-development are vital. In order to find out how far you have developed it is important to look where you started from. A skills audit is a useful way of looking at where you are now. You can then decide where you want to be and plan how to get there.

If you are working on this section at the start of the course, you will be able to list your skills and knowledge quite easily. If, however, you are part way through the course, you may have to remember what it was like when you started.

Activity 11

Linking to P2.
Look at the sample Jay completed, then make a blank checklist and fill in your details at the start of the course. Keep a copy so that you can add to it halfway through the course and then at the end to see how you have progressed.

JAY B	AT THE START OF THE COURSE	HALFWAY THROUGH	AT THE END OF THE COURSE
Current knowledge	I've heard of the NHS but I don't know these new words like 'policy' and 'accountability'.	I've used the website www.dfes.gov.uk to find what the government is going to do about helping young people. The Green Paper 'Youth Matters' has some good suggestions.	People who work in health and social care must stand up for the rights of vulnerable people. I listen to the news and keep up to date with changes for young people in care. If I don't agree, I talk to my local member of parliament.

Activity 11 (continued)

JAY B	AT THE START OF THE COURSE	HALFWAY THROUGH	AT THE END OF THE COURSE
Skills	My strengths are that I'm friendly, I like people, I understand what it's like to get into trouble. Someone from my family is on probation. My weak areas? I don't know.	My weak areas are writing assignments and getting the work in on time. My strengths are that I get good reports from placement and get on well with the rest of my group.	I've improved my time management and get all my assignments in on time, but I still don't enjoy writing. I really liked my last placement and I'm volunteering as a mentor for young people.
Values	I think everyone should be treated the same. We are all equal.	Treating everyone the same isn't being equal. Some people like to be independent and do things for themselves. Others cannot and need more help.	We should treat everyone with respect. I should ask what help they need before I make assumptions.
Beliefs	I believe asylum seekers should be sent back to their own country.	I met an asylum seeker when I went on placement. She had been raped in her own village and her father was killed trying to defend her. Perhaps not everyone should be sent back.	Every case is different and every person is different. We should not judge until we know the facts.
Career aspirations	I'm not sure what social workers do but I think I would like to be one. I've seen them on the television and it looks a good job. I don't know how to become a social worker.	I know I have to go to university to become a social worker. I know there is a code of conduct and a General Social Care Council. At my placement, I talked to a social worker about the job. I didn't realise they have to be on call at weekends.	Social work is very stressful. I don't like a lot of stress. There is also a lot of paperwork which I don't like. I can help young people if I become a youth worker. I can go to university and do that.

Activity 11 (continued)

JAY B	AT THE START OF THE COURSE	HALFWAY THROUGH	AT THE END OF THE COURSE
Self-awareness	I know what I look like. Is that what it means?	My placement report said I was often late. I should get up earlier because I really enjoy it when I'm there.	I got a good report from my last placement because I took their advice and worked on my weak areas. I go to bed a bit earlier so I can catch the early bus. They've even offered me a job when I finish my course!

It is impossible to include everything in a review. Jay included the things important to her. If you follow a section along, you can see how Jay developed personally, by accepting criticism of her lateness and doing something about it. You can see how she developed professionally, from knowing very little about social care work to getting involved with representing the views of young people.

The audit is a general overview. Sometimes we need a more detailed plan. Action plans come in several forms. The simplest plan is a three-stage model. It asks:

- Where am I now?
- Where do I want to be?
- How do I get there?

Rehan used this model to help with gaps in his current knowledge. He started with the first step: Where am I now? Here is his list:

- Where am I now? A bit lost! I don't understand these words:
  current
  contemporary
  values
  beliefs
  skills
- Where do I want to be? I want to understand what people are talking about.
- How do I get there?

What suggestions can you make to help Rehan? Here are some ideas:

- use a paper-based dictionary
- use the dictionary on Tools, Language, and Thesaurus
- ask the tutor
- make a list in your diary and learn a new word every day

When Rehan looked at the meaning of 'current' and 'contemporary', he found they mean the same thing – 'modern'.

Don't be scared of words. If you see a new word, look it up, then you can use it!

So how do you find out about current knowledge and skills?

- Use up-to-date journals and official websites.
- Make a list of theories and legislation. Summarise them on index cards. Colour code them, so you might have blue for legislation, white for theories.
- Make mind maps so you have legislation on one page, theories on another.
- Organise your file so you can find information quickly.

Where can I find out about careers?

- There is a dedicated website for NHS careers. See www.nhscareers.nhs.uk to find out about careers such as speech and language therapy, art therapy as well as the usual nursing and midwifery careers.
- The department of health has a website for social work careers. See www.socialworkandcare.co.uk/socialwork for social work jobs and social work as a career.

What skills do I need to work in health and social care?

Communication is the key skill which enables us to do our job. A health care worker who does not speak the language of the service user is limited in what they can do, so if you work with people with a hearing impairment, you may need to learn British Sign Language if that is their main language.

Most communication is non-verbal. People read visual clues and rely on instinct even if you say the opposite, so if a service user asks you whether you smoke, be honest – your body language will tell the truth.

Team work is essential in care work. No one can care effectively without others. A doctor needs a nurse to tell him or her whether a patient has had pain. A nurse needs the care assistant to report any changes. Team work saves lives. There is no room for temper tantrums in care work. Good carers get along with everyone even if they don't like them.

Did you know?

The Matchbox Café in Birmingham is run by people with learning disabilities. Their enablers help them to learn skills such as preparing food, operating a till and taking food hygiene courses.

The Matchbox Café

Technical skills range from using computers to craft work. A social worker may help a child make a life story book, sticking pictures in an album. A care worker may help a person with a stroke to regain muscle tone by playing hand ball. An art therapist may help someone with depression to express their feelings. Care work is varied. You have to be flexible and willing to learn new skills.

Research skills are increasingly important, especially if you intend to go to university. You will be used to using secondary sources for your assignments, but may be less experienced with primary research and data handling. These skills will be developed as you study at a higher level. Computerised data-handling packages are used now at university, but you need to understand the data!

Personal skills are important in every job. A disorganised person may be creative but will not get very far if they miss deadlines or do not complete work. A professional must be organised in their work or service users suffer. A social worker who cannot find the notes for a service user review is not doing the best for the service user. A service user who has a chaotic lifestyle will not put much faith in a social worker who is equally chaotic.

Personal presentation matters. People do judge by first appearances. A social worker dressed in a formal suit will not build up rapport with a young runaway, but might impress a panel of judges. Personal presentation should be suited to the situation, but no one respects a professional care worker who is dirty or smelly or who swears.

Practice in care is underpinned by the care value base, sometimes called the principles of caring. These are:

- promoting anti-discriminatory practice
- maintaining the confidentiality of information
- promoting and supporting individuals' rights and choices
- acknowledging personal beliefs and identity
- ensuring effective communication.

A professional care worker must not impose their views on others, but must listen and put forward the views of service users, even if they do not share those views. A social worker who disapproves of drugs cannot discriminate against drug addicts. A nurse who does not believe in abortion cannot impose their views on a pregnant woman.

The standards expected of professionals are high. Case studies from the Nursing and Midwifery Council website illustrate what can go wrong when professional standards are lost. In both the following cases, the professional had their name removed from the relevant register.

Case Study 1

The Professional Conduct Committee considered the case of a community psychiatric nurse who faced one charge of having a sexual relationship with a patient (Ms A). The practitioner was present at the hearing and was represented by a solicitor. He admitted the charge and that it amounted to professional misconduct.

Case Study 2

The Professional Conduct Committee heard the case of a registered nurse and midwife, who was working as an 'F' grade core midwife in a hospital environment. The practitioner faced three allegations, including failure to obtain medical assistance or to contact the senior midwife for a patient who had high risk factors, failure to keep adequate records of care for the same patient (particularly with regards to observations and fluid balance charts and medication records) and failure to undertake the proper transfer of care to the oncoming midwife.

(Source: Nursing and Midwifery Council)

Activity 12

Linking to P7.
What do you think? Should professionals be accountable for the care they give? Or do we expect too much?
Debate this in your group. One person should represent the case for accountability and one person should represent the case against accountability.

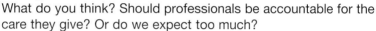

Plan for your own development

This section looks at setting targets to assist your personal and professional development.

For this unit and as a future professional, you will have to plan and set targets and goals which will enable you to develop as a professional. A development plan is often a requirement of workers within health and social care organisations.

Targets could be in relation to different issues within personal and professional development. The setting of targets and goals provides a benchmark against which future development can be measured. Goals can be short term or long term. Short-term targets are those which you can realistically achieve within 3–6 months. An example would be to improve your knowledge of policies and procedures within the workplace. Goals can also be long term (which can take up to 18 months or longer). An example could be to develop effective communication skills with a variety of service users or learning new skills such as British Sign Language.

Your goals should be personal to you and relate to health and social care. These goals should be decided upon by looking at areas that you wish to or need to develop and improve. Once you have decided upon your targets, you need to consider the steps that should be taken to achieve these.

Setting targets

Targets you set for yourself should be achievable within the time you have and the resources available. If your targets are too ambitious, you may become demotivated. If your targets are achievable and you complete them, this will increase your sense of achievement. When setting targets they should be 'SMART'.

- **S**pecific
- **M**easureable
- **A**ctionable
- **R**elevant
- **T**imely

Targets should be specific – the goal should focus on a definite area. It should be exact and unambiguous.

You must consider how you are going to measure your results.

- How will you know you have achieved your goals?
- Is the goal you have set realistic?
- Can you achieve it?
- Is the goal you have set yourself related to the area you are studying?
- Have you set yourself the right amount of time to achieve your goals?
  Consider whether you might need a bit more or a bit less time than you think.

Activity 13

Ahmed wants to increase his knowledge of health and safety legislation. He has a work placement and also has the option of attending a health and safety one-day course. Set Ahmed some targets to achieve over two months that will meet his goal. Make sure they are SMART.

Personal goals

There are different goals that you may wish to set as your long- or short-term targets. These should reflect your areas highlighted for development. Some possible examples are shown opposite.

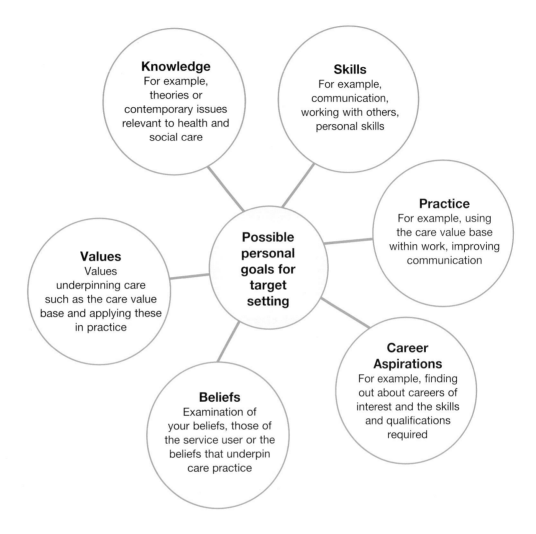

Knowledge
For example, theories or contemporary issues relevant to health and social care

Skills
For example, communication, working with others, personal skills

Practice
For example, using the care value base within work, improving communication

Values
Values underpinning care such as the care value base and applying these in practice

Possible personal goals for target setting

Career Aspirations
For example, finding out about careers of interest and the skills and qualifications required

Beliefs
Examination of your beliefs, those of the service user or the beliefs that underpin care practice

Activity 14

Linking to P3.
Using your self-assessment, choose targets that will act as your long- or short-term targets. Give reasons for your choices. How will improvement in these areas help you in your future career?

Monitoring and evaluating your plan in relation to your own development

Once you have chosen your targets, it is important that you monitor your progress on a regular basis. This can ensure that you are still on track and can alter or do more as necessary. This also helps guarantee that you will not end up in 18 months' time without any targets achieved. You could monitor your progress in a table format such as the one on the next page.

TARGET	DATE OF MEETING	WORK TOWARDS ACHIEVING THIS (WITH REFERENCE)	WORK STILL TO DO	DATE OF NEXT MEETING	REFERENCE FOR ACHIEVE-MENT
To familiarise and use work placement	20.9.07	Received policy pack from placement and read through	Attend health and safety training (due 31.9.07). Receive placement supervisions	1.10.07	Notes made on policies
	1.10.07	Have attended health and safety training (see certificate)	Receive placement supervisions and put theory into practice	1.11.07	Health and safety certificate

You could also record this as individual steps working towards achieving a specific goal. For example:

Target: To Improve Communication Skills

STEP	TARGET DATE	ACHIEVED	REFERENCE FOR EVIDENCE
Study – Unit 1 Communication	13.10.07	13.10.07 ✓	Feedback on assignment
Practice communication within class and receive feedback	13.11.07	10.11.07	Witness statements
Be observed communicating within class and receive feedback	14.12.07		
Act on feedback received			

By regularly monitoring your progress you will meet your goals and targets. When monitoring you should look at what you have achieved and what else you need to undertake to meet your targets. As you progress through the course, you may find that you need to make changes. This could be due to your own development needs or wanting to pursue different goals to meet your targets. You may find that you achieve your targets sooner or later than you anticipated. However, if you find that you are diverting from your targets significantly, this needs to be addressed. You may also find that you need to change the development plan as a response to your reflections upon a situation. You can then ascertain your feeling of progress and change your plan accordingly.

Contexts of development

There are different situations that may provide valuable evidence for your portfolio. You may be able to use all of these or just a couple. It is important to remember that it is the recognition of the skills obtained and reflecting and then using these in practice that is central to developing as a professional.

Work experience placement

Attending your placement is a compulsory element of your course. Here you can put the theory you have learned into practice. For example, you may have learned about how to offer service users choices, such as food to eat, clothes to wear or activities. Within placement you may have the opportunity to carry this out in practice. This will help you achieve your goals and meet your targets.

It is imperative that you keep a record of your placement and the activities you undertake. This should also be reflective, which will enable you to look back upon the situation and decide what your strengths and weaknesses are and identify opportunities for development.

Visits

As part of your course, you may also go on visits to care settings. Use these as an opportunity to compare your placement to the way the care setting practises or to ask questions, reflect on the visit and therefore add evidence to your portfolio.

Study environment

Your study and the environment within which you study can help you to develop the skills necessary to achieve on the course. You may gain valuable experiences from the units, the lessons or your own research. You should ensure that you keep this information safe and record as you go along. You may also like to reflect upon your study skills and how these develop over the two years.

Life events

Events may occur within the course of your life that you can reflect upon and add in as evidence within your portfolio. For example, it could be an occasion when you have to access health and social care services. You would then be seeing this service from a service user perspective. This may then go on to influence how you practise and therefore impact upon the care you give.

Other events

Other events may assist you in gaining evidence for your portfolio. This may include employment that you undertake outside of your work placement. You can use this to compare and contrast policies and procedures in your placement or to develop new skills or improve your existing ones.

Activity 15

Linking to P4.
Think about the contexts that you work in at the moment.
What evidence do you think you will be able to get from them?

Professional development portfolio

Over the next two years you will assemble a wealth of evidence to include in your portfolio. You will have to consider how you are going to present this information. It must be organised and all the information should be easily accessible. Your portfolio should include the following:

- Professional practice log book. You should complete a log showing attendance and reflection on your experiences.
- Variety of contexts: reflecting on a variety of contexts will give you great scope from which to draw evidence.
- Authenticated records: including your genuine records will validate your portfolio and demonstrate progression.
- Indexing: this will help you locate the information required and also allow the assessor to identify the evidence that meets your targets.
- Structured: your portfolio should follow a logical order and be planned and organised.

Collecting relevant evidence

There is a wide variety of evidence that you can include in your portfolio. It is essential that you collect this as you go along to ensure that you are not left assembling a two-year portfolio in two months!

Evidence can be formal, which is the official evidence, or informal, which comprises a less official way to approach evidence. Some examples are given overleaf.

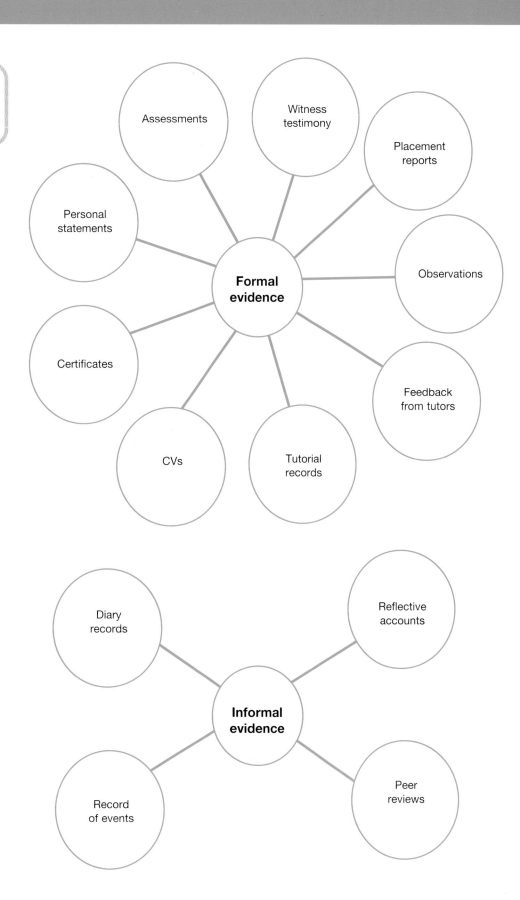

Remember

Collect as you go!

Assessments

Witness testimony

Placement reports

Personal statements

Formal evidence

Observations

Certificates

Feedback from tutors

CVs

Tutorial records

Diary records

Reflective accounts

Informal evidence

Record of events

Peer reviews

Types of formal evidence

Assessments

These may take the form of assignments or evidence. They can demonstrate your understanding of topics and you can include them as part of your assessment for this unit. For example, if your target was to improve your communication skills, then your evidence from your interactions in Unit 1 may provide evidence towards achieving this goal. Assessment can also be obtained from your manager at your work placement – for example an appraisal. Assessment may also be given from service users. This is an important aspect of assessment and if you are able to obtain this, it will be useful evidence in your portfolio.

Observations

Observations may take place within classroom activities or as part of your placement. Examples of observations may include conversations with service users or activities you have undertaken.

Witness testimony

If you undertake any observations from placement, a witness statement can provide evidence for this. Ensure that any testimony is dated and signed by your supervisor. It should also contain details of the activity that you undertake.

Placement reports

Your placement supervisor will speak to your tutor about your progress. This can demonstrate an improvement in the skills that you may have achieved or your ability to carry out a certain task. If there is a specific goal you have set yourself, you may like to ask your tutor or placement supervisor to report on this to demonstrate your achievement.

Feedback from tutors

Feedback may be any time and could be in relation to a specific event or following an assignment. You may like to use this evidence towards completing your portfolio if it is relevant.

Tutorial records

Tutorial records can provide invaluable evidence. They can demonstrate your achievement and progression towards certain goals. Your tutor can also set you particular goals which may help you achieve your targets for Unit 6.

CV

Your curriculum vitae is a valuable source of evidence and can display your current skills. You could include a CV at the start and end of the course to demonstrate your progression.

Personal statement

Personal statements are often used to provide more evidence for jobs or university applications. This can show your aptitude and provide an invaluable opportunity for you to demonstrate your ability. Sell yourself!

Certificates

Certificates that might provide evidence for your portfolio include GCSE results, first aid, food hygiene or health and safety.

Types of informal evidence

Diary records

You should keep a record or diary that reflects your contribution and the role that you take within placement.

Peer reviews

Peer reviews are when you receive feedback about something from your colleagues or fellow students. This can sometimes be used in assessments with managers or tutors. It is important to ensure that the feedback you may give to someone is constructive and carried out privately.

Reflective accounts

A reflective account provides thoughts and feelings about events that occurred and enables you to look back at them and decide whether you have learned anything new or whether there are areas that you need to develop or gaps in your knowledge. This can assist you looking at your progression as a professional. Remember to try to be honest with yourself. It will be you who loses out otherwise.

Record of events

A record of events will give you key dates of when you carried out activities. It will then be easy to cross-reference evidence you have collected.

Remember

When collecting evidence or asking for feedback, be clear about what it is you are looking for. What are you trying to prove, i.e. evidence towards achieving your targets?

Activity 16

Make a list of the evidence you can collect now and the evidence you may collect in the next few months. Which of your targets would the evidence meet?

Support for development

There are a number of sources of support for your development. These include tutors, peers, supervisors and mentors. When receiving support, make sure that both you and the person delivering it have the time to provide you with the feedback.

Tutors

Tutors at college can direct you towards meeting your targets. Your tutor can guide you towards progression and achievement.

Peers

Peers can provide support for your development and you can support your peers. This may occur on an informal basis, which means you may not even realise you are supporting each other's development. This may be through offering advice to each other on aspects of work, or giving guidance on how to do something. There is also valuable support to be gained through encouraging each other and providing emotional support. Do not forget that your peers may be the people you work with in placement.

Supervisors

A supervisor tends to be a professional within your workplace who will have responsibility for day-to-day supervision. A supervisor will often meet with you on a one-to-one basis to assist you in developing your practice. They will tend to focus on how you are developing as a worker and how this relates to your practice. To maximise the use of supervision it is often helpful if you understand your role and the needs of the service users. You can then compare this to the roles that the organisation has and ascertain areas for development.

Mentors

A mentor system exists in health and social care to support people when they start work. If you have a mentor within placement they can provide support to assist development.

Meetings

Any meetings that you participate in should be planned. It is essential that you have an agenda of issues that you wish to cover. A team meeting may look at issues such as concerns about service users or planned activities. If the meeting is to discuss your progress, ideally it should be more than just a discussion of your progress; it should look at how you move forward as a professional.

Information can be obtained from a wide variety of sources, including news, books, TV programmes as well as your supervisors and colleagues. There are continually new developments within health and social care and these will impact upon your work at some point. You should begin to take responsibility to keep up to date with new developments and current thinking on practice and then use these within practice.

Activity 17

Read a newspaper or watch the television news for a week. Whenever there are references to new research or development within health and social care, make a note of these. Discuss them within class and consider the possible implications for placement.

Remember

The principles of good care practice never change – treating people with dignity, respecting their rights and producing the best care possible.

Reflecting on your own development

Reflective practice is an integral part of health and social care practice. It is considered helpful to reflect on health and social care experiences to improve practice. This therefore helps us to learn.

Reflective practice can be considered as 'thinking things over'. There are many approaches to learning through reflective practice.

Donald Schön considered that professionals achieve advanced levels of effective judgement and decision making by developing reflective skills. They get better at their job by reflecting. In *The Reflective Practitioner*, he considered two different times when you might use reflective practice:

● *Reflect in practice*. This is when you are involved in a situation and you reflect on it at the time. You are thinking on your feet. You have to access a wide range of personal knowledge rapidly.
● *Reflect on practice*. This occurs after the situation has taken place and you reflect on it then. You think things over at your leisure and build your knowledge or understanding.

For more information, see Smith, M.K. (2001) *Donald Schön: learning, reflection and change* and *The Encyclopaedia of Informal Education* at www.infed.org/thinkers/et-schon.htm.

Schön has been criticised by some for the following:

● His definition and times when you would reflect are considered 'narrow'. He considered only practical experience.
● It therefore does not provide a means to use material that is not gathered as 'new' (e.g. a course) or learned from other situations (e.g. what someone tells you).

Jennifer Moon (2001: 51) states that Schön did not define what he meant by 'real world practice' (this is what you reflect on). Moon has also produced her own stages of reflective practice.

A piece of writing that is reflective is not just a description of what happened. Reflective writing involves actively looking back at the situation. Your conclusions can then provide a guide to your own practice next time.

Remember, reflective practice is not about making you feel bad about yourself or being over critical, as this is unhelpful. You need to look at your practice and decide where you need to go to carry out additional development.

In order to reflect effectively it is important to 'know yourself'. You need to understand your own values, interests and priorities. These all have an impact upon your practice and it is important to acknowledge this.

Linking theory into practice

During your time on the course you will learn about a lot of different theories. These theories provide models of how care practice should be undertaken. To develop as a practitioner you should try out these theories in practice. For example, you may learn how to communicate effectively with people or how to keep people safe within the workplace or community. You can then try out the communication skills you have learned within a classroom situation. This is known as linking theory into practice. You can then think about how well this went and what aspects you still need to develop.

It might not always be successful, but making mistakes or activities not going according to plan are ways of learning. You should consider why something did not go according to plan and how this may be improved upon next time. However, do not forget that real and sometimes vulnerable people will be on the receiving end of any mistakes. Therefore if you do not feel confident in undertaking an activity or carrying out something with a service user or service user, talk to your supervisor and ask not to do it.

Seeing the care value base in practice gives you the opportunity to reflect and see why it is important.

Learning about care value base. What the care values are and why they are important.

Opportunity to use and apply the care value base within your work placement.

Activity 18

Try to answer the reflective questions using an example from your placement.

Keeping a reflective diary will help identify the links between theory and practice. It will assist you in looking at your placement, linking theory into practice and identifying areas for development.

Some questions when reflecting are:

- What happened?
- Did you have a plan before undertaking the activity or the incident you are writing about?
- How do you feel about what happened?
- Do you need to make any adjustment?
- Have you learned any new skills?
- If you were to do this again, what would you do differently?
- What would you do the same?
- Do you need any support or to learn new skills before this occurs again?

Example of reflective writing

Today I was taking A out on an activity. As we were getting ready, A became aggressive and went into the kitchen and broke a plate. I felt quite shocked at this as I have not seen it before. It made me feel quite stressed and a little bit frightened.

My line manager was there, who handled the situation. She spoke to A and he calmed down. The line manager spoke to A in a clear, calm voice. We then spoke about the incident and talked about possible triggers for this. My supervisor and I think that he became anxious as he had to wait for another service user to get ready. In future I will wait until the other service user is ready before assisting A. This will mean he does not have to wait as long. I still feel a bit wary about being around A, but I know that it was not a reaction to me but a communication of his anxiety levels.

Influence of personal values and beliefs

Activity 19

What values and beliefs do you have?

As an individual you will have your own values and beliefs. These may come from many influences, such as the media, the way you were brought up, your religion or what you find important.

The personal values and beliefs you hold may have a positive or negative impact upon the care you give to people. You may not always realise this occurs. For example, see the following table:

YOUR VALUE/ BELIEF	YOUR SERVICE USER'S VALUE/ BELIEF	HOW BEING AROUND THE SERVICE USER MAKES YOU FEEL	IMPACT UPON CARE
You like hip-hop music and the latest chart. You do not like classical music.	Your service user likes classical music and opera.	Listening to music you do not like makes you feel stressed and you do not really like listening to it.	You may rush your job or not pay full attention to your service user as you are thinking about how much you do not like the music.

Activity 20

Now try to complete the following:

YOUR VALUE/ BELIEF	YOUR SERVICE USER'S VALUE/BELIEF	HOW BEING AROUND THE SERVICE USER MAKES YOU FEEL	IMPACT UPON CARE
You have strong views on animal rights.	That fox hunting is fine and he eats meat with every meal.		

Being aware of your own values and beliefs means you can identify how these impact upon practice. You can then explore these views in supervision or tutorials to ensure the effects on care are limited.

3 Understand service provision in the health or social care sectors

Health and social care in the UK is provided by different sectors. Private care is paid for by the people using the services, while statutory health care is provided by the government. This is funded through taxes. Examples of this are the National Health Service (NHS) and the Social Services.

Informal care is provided by friends and family. They are not paid, yet are often a crucial part of health care provision. Carers UK estimates that every day another 6000 people take on a caring role. For more information go to www.carersuk.org.

Voluntary care comes from non-profit-making organisations. These are numerous and include ChildLine, the NSPCC and Age Concern.

Activity 21

Working with a partner, research a voluntary/non-profit-making organisation. Display your information on a poster to present to the class.
Or
Look at carers within the UK. What extra assistance and support would they need? Where might they get this help?

Activity 22

Find your nearest NHS walk-in centre and other primary health care professionals.

Accessing health and social care services

A GP is the first person many people see about a health problem. This is known as primary health care. Other primary care providers include dentists, NHS Direct, pharmacists and NHS walk-in centres.

- NHS Direct offers a 24-hour telephone and e-health service. See www.nhsdirect.nhs.uk
- NHS walk-in centres are present in local areas and offer access to a range of health information services. They offer advice and treatment. See www.nhs.uk/england/ noAppointmentNeeded/walkinCentres.

If a health problem cannot be resolved through primary care, you will be referred to secondary care. This may be hospital or day surgery. If you need specialist long-term care such as rehabilitative treatment, this is known as tertiary care.

Activity 23

Find out how your placement is funded. Which sector does this relate to? Compare this with others in your group/class.

The NHS

The NHS is continually changing in structure and provision.

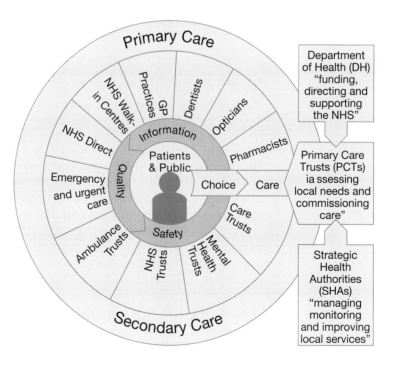

Source: www.nhs.uk

Primary Care Trusts (PCTs)

These control 80 per cent of the NHS budget. They are local organisations and consequently can understand the needs of the people in their area. This also means that resources can be tailored to meet these needs. PCTs report to the strategic health authorities (SHAs). The strategic health authorities monitor how well PCTs and hospitals are doing and will address any problems that arise. There are ten SHAs and they link the PCTs to the Department of Health.

Department of Health

This is the government department responsible for improving the health and well-being of people in England. It will set the direction for the NHS to follow and provide the funding to do this.

NHS trusts

Hospitals are managed by trusts. They make sure that hospitals provide high-quality care and that they spend money efficiently. They employ the majority of the workforce, from hospital consultants to support staff.

Ambulance trusts

There are currently 13 ambulance trusts which are responsible for responding to 999 calls in emergency situations. Ambulance trusts also assist the NHS in providing transport for patients to attend hospital appointments.

Mental health trusts

These provide care for service users with mental health problems. They provide a range of services, including specialist care.

Social services

Social services look after the welfare of people. There are many service user groups that may access social services, including those with disabilities or older people.

Social services are run by local authorities, so each local area has its own social services office. In recent years the partnership between health and social services has grown, so frequently these organisations will work together.

Local health/social care provider

Each area of the country has specific health or social care services. Each of these will have a specific type of provision and will be funded in a certain way.

Barriers to access

A barrier is something that stops you from doing something. Within health and social care, this involves you being stopped from accessing health and social care services. This can be for a number of reasons. Read the following case study and identify the barriers.

Case Study
Gareth

Gareth lives in a rural area with limited access to health and social care services. He does not have much money and therefore cannot afford taxis to the nearby towns. The buses are limited and run only early in the morning or late in the evening.

Gareth lives next door to a woman who is a Muslim. As part of her religion she prefers being treated by a Muslim doctor. However, they are underrepresented within the locality.

Gareth's wife Susan has discovered a lump. She is very concerned that it may be cancer. However, she is too scared to go to the doctor.

Activity 24

For each of the barriers you have identified in the Gareth case study, how could these be overcome?

Barriers to access may be as a result of the geographical locality and where the service user lives. They may also be a result of individual preferences or as a consequence of social and cultural reasons. People may have financial difficulties or not be able to understand the language. As professionals it is important to be aware of these barriers and to try to break them down as much as possible. This could be through bringing services into the community or awareness-raising campaigns to reduce fears and concerns about accessing treatment.

Understanding the influences that shape contemporary health and social care service

Health and social care workers

The health and social care sector requires many people undertaking a variety of job roles. All of these roles are fundamental to developing good care practice. Each job is important. The diagram on the next page illustrates how these roles may be considered.

Health and Social Care professionals.
All professionals have a role to play in promoting a successful sector. Here are some examples.

| Professionals e.g. nursing and social workers. | Professionals allied to medicine. These are key members of the health care team and include physiotherapists and psychologists | Technical support. These professionals play a vital role in assisting and supporting the work of those within health and social care. | Other support professionals. There are also professionals who play a vital role in health and social care. These include administrators and clerks. |

There are often different ways you can qualify for each of these jobs. When considering a profession you should look at what the job involves and if there is more than one entry route, which one suits you best.

Case Study

Mark is an art therapist and works for the psychiatric unit of a local hospital. His role is to help service users communicate their emotions. He has an arts degree and a postgraduate qualification.

Jodie is a phlebotomist, which means she collects blood to help diagnose diseases. She left school with GCSEs and was trained within the workplace. Jodie now takes blood from people across a range of ages, including children and older people, and also transports them to be tested.

Activity 25

In small groups, choose one job from each of the branches.
Research the qualifications and skills needed to qualify for this job.
Use www.nhscareers.nhs.uk or Connexions Direct to help. You careers officer will also have some useful information.

Workforce development

Health and social care, like any other profession, is continually changing. New techniques are learned and new ways of doing things are used. It is part of the role of a health and social care professional to keep up to date with these techniques. You may go on courses and receive updates. You can also access this information from professional journals or magazines. This is sometimes known as continuing professional development and professional competence. As part of your placement, you may go on courses. You can include these as evidence in your portfolio.

Remember that being well educated and up to date can lead to a higher level of service.

Activity 26

What other benefits are there from continuing your professional development? (Think of physical, intellectual, emotional and social benefits as well as those that benefit the service users.)

The Sector Skills Council for Health

The aim of the Sector Skills Council is to help develop a skilled workforce within health care.

Develop and manage national workforce competencies	Leading and facilitating the development, maintenance and use of national workforce competence frameworks, embracing National Occupational Standards, and evaluating their impact and use
Profile the UK workforce	Bringing together Labour Market Intelligence for the whole UK health sector
Identify and articulate sector workforce needs	Working with and on behalf of a network of employers in the Nations and Regions of the UK
Improve workforce skills	Developing and implementing a strategy for skills escalation embracing the use of qualifications and career frameworks
Influence education and training supply	Ensuring the sector gets the skills it wants through influencing learning supply by developing a 'Sector Skills Agreement.' Developing employer-led partnership approaches to quality assurance of education and training
Work with our partners	Working in a focussed and strategic way with key partners, stakeholders and customers across the sector

Source: www.skillsforhealth.org.uk

There are other workforce development activities that help contribute to a competent workforce. These include National Occupational Standards and monitoring performance of workers through activities such as appraisal.

Role of professional bodies

Within health and social care, there are professional bodies set up by the government. Their role is to protect the public. Registration is often a requirement before you can work in that field. Examples include the General Social Care Council (www.gscc.org.uk) and the Nursing and Midwifery Council (www.nmc-uk.org).

The professional bodies keep a register of competent professionals and in serious cases of misconduct a professional will be struck off the register. By being on the register you are agreeing to abide by the codes of conduct issued by that professional body. They also provide advice to members of the profession and will consider allegations of misconduct or people who are unfit to practise. (Source: www.gscc.org.uk/NR/rdonlyres/041E6261-6BB0-43A7-A9A4-80F658D2A0B4/0/Codes_of_Practice.pdf)

Activity 27

Make a leaflet aimed at members of the public which includes the role of professional bodies and which professional body relates to which job.

The NMC code of professional conduct: standards for conduct, performance and ethics

As a registered nurse, midwife or specialist community public health nurse, you are personally accountable for your practice. In caring for patients and clients, you must:

- respect the patient or client as an individual
- obtain consent before you give any treatment or care
- protect confidential information
- co-operate with others in the team
- maintain your professional knowledge and competence
- be trustworthy
- act to identify and minimise risk to patients and clients.

These are the shared values of all the United Kingdom health care regulatory bodies.

(Extract from the NMC code of conduct.)

Codes of conduct

Many professional bodies publish codes of conduct. These codes provide guidance on how as a professional you should behave. Many professions will have their own code of conduct. Nurses and midwifes follow the Nursing and Midwifery Code of Practice, Social Workers the General Social Care Council Code of Practice.

Activity 28

Research another professional body's code of conduct. Put this information on a poster and share your information with the rest of the class.

Roles and responsibilities

As a professional you will have your role to play within health and social care. You will also have responsibilities towards your patients, your employers and the profession. Professionals should actively support their service users and empower them. Service users can then be as independent as possible. Although each individual job is unique, general rules are to respect your service users and their wishes, maintain confidentiality, foster equality and diversity and promote the rights of service users.

Multi-disciplinary work

Multi-disciplinary work means many professionals working together. This has benefits because each discipline can bring its own skills and expertise. Multi-disciplinary work pools resources and can reduce duplication of services.

Activity 29

Look at each of the following job roles: social worker, support worker, health visitor, occupational therapist.
What skills and expertise could they offer?

SUMMARY

- It is important that you collect sources of evidence to put in your file and to develop your portfolio as you go.

- You can access a wealth of support from tutors, peers and within placement.

- Reflective practice is an important aspect of care.

- Our personal values and beliefs can have an impact upon care practice.

- Health and social care provision is funded in different ways and there are a variety of services and providers.

- Barriers exist which may prevent people from accessing health and social care services.

- Many professionals make up the workforce, offering skills and expertise in the care they provide to service users.

Grading grid

In order to pass this unit, the evidence that the learner presents for assessment needs to demonstrate that they can meet all of the learning outcomes for the unit. The criteria for a pass grade describe the level of achievement required to pass this unit.

GRADING CRITERIA

TO ACHIEVE A PASS GRADE THE EVIDENCE MUST SHOW THAT THE LEARNER IS ABLE TO:	TO ACHIEVE A MERIT GRADE THE EVIDENCE MUST SHOW THAT, IN ADDITION TO THE PASS CRITERIA, THE LEARNER IS ABLE TO:	TO ACHIEVE A DISTINCTION GRADE THE EVIDENCE MUST SHOW THAT, IN ADDITION TO THE PASS AND MERIT CRITERIA, THE LEARNER IS ABLE TO:
P1 explain key influences on personal learning processes of individuals	M1 analyse the impact of key influences on personal learning processes on own learning	D1 evaluate how personal learning and development may benefit others
P2 describe own knowledge, skills, practice, values, beliefs and career aspirations at start of programme		
P3 produce and monitor an action plan for self-development and the achievement of own personal goals		
P4 describe own progress against action plan over the duration of the programme	M2 explain how the action plan has helped support own development over the duration of the programme	D2 evaluate own development over the duration of the programme.

GRADING CRITERIA

TO ACHIEVE A PASS GRADE THE EVIDENCE MUST SHOW THAT THE LEARNER IS ABLE TO:	TO ACHIEVE A MERIT GRADE THE EVIDENCE MUST SHOW THAT, IN ADDITION TO THE PASS CRITERIA, THE LEARNER IS ABLE TO:	TO ACHIEVE A DISTINCTION GRADE THE EVIDENCE MUST SHOW THAT, IN ADDITION TO THE PASS AND MERIT CRITERIA, THE LEARNER IS ABLE TO:
P5 produce and reflect on own personal and professional development portfolio	M3 reflect on own experiences and use three examples to explain links between theory and practice.	
P6 describe one local health or social care service provider and identify its place in national provision		
P7 describe the roles, responsibilities and career pathways of three health or social care workers.		

This unit provides an introduction to society. Sociology is a way of investigating and explaining society. Sociology for health looks at the way in which we define health and wellbeing and also examines the health inequalities and explanations for these.

Learning Outcomes

On completion of this unit you should be able to:

1 Understand sociological approaches to study
2 Apply sociological approaches to health and social care

1 Understand sociological approaches to study

Sociology is concerned with the way individuals and groups operate within society and the way in which groups interact with each other. There are different sociological perspectives which provide different models of society.

TERMINOLOGY		
SOCIAL STRUCTURES	SOCIAL DIVERSITY	SOCIALISATION
Sociologists generally see society as being organised through social institutions. These include the family, education and health care services. Sociologists consider that each of these has a role in society.	Diversity is the way that people are different from one another. This includes age, gender, culture, ethnicity and location.	This is the process through which people learn the norms and values of society. **Norms** are social rules about what is important in society. **Values** are what are important to an individual or social group. **Beliefs** are what an individual or group accept as true. **Roles** are the responsibility and functions of someone or a body. **Status** is the importance placed upon someone or something. **Socialisation** is gained through parents, friends, family, media and society itself.

Activity 1

What norms, values and beliefs do you and society have? How do these compare with other societies? What influences are there on your values and beliefs?

Principal sociological perspectives

This section looks at different theories of sociology and how they view society. Theories are ways of looking at something – for example, society. All of the theories concentrate on society but have different ways of looking at it.

Activity 2

Use a pair of binoculars to look at an object and note what you see. Now turn the binoculars around and look at the same object again. You are seeing the same object but in a different way. This is the same as sociological theories. They are all looking at aspects of society but will have different perspectives.

Sociological theory can be divided into two different types:

● macro – human activity is seen as a result of social structures
● micro – smaller groups of people interact with each other

Functionalism

Key people – Emile Durkheim (1858–1917): French sociologist, often referred to as the Father of Sociology, who was instrumental in establishing sociology as a science; *Talcott Parsons* (1902–1979), US sociologist.

Functionalism looks at social structures by the role they have in society. It considers that each social structure is essential for the interests of society.

For example, a flower has many parts. Each part is essential to its wellbeing – without it the flower will not survive. This is the same for functionalism.

Functionalism considers that humans and societies have basic needs, and institutions are seen in terms of the contribution that they make to meeting these needs and therefore society. It believes there are forces which limit individual behaviour. This means that there is order within society and this is based on all individuals having the same values. Functionalism does recognise that there is inequality within society but considers this functional for society.

There have been criticisms of functionalism. It looks at social structures in society while ignoring individuals and the fact that individuals have their own choices. It ignores conflict and diversity. Functionalism tries to see everything as positive and having a function. Factors such as inequality are seen as functional to society; they are helpful to the running of society. People are given rewards if they do well (such as higher wages and better status) and this acts as an incentive for people to work hard and train, which in turn means that the more skilled people will do jobs and hold positions seen as crucial within society.

Marxism

Karl Marx

Key person – Karl Marx: German philosopher, often called the Father of Communism.

Marxism is a structuralist theory which considers that society is based on conflicts of interests. It stresses the importance of the role of conflict. Economics is at the basis of social life and progress is made through the struggle between social classes. The ruling class is based on ownership.

Social change is the result of class struggle. Under Marxism, economic (financial) structures and systems and social class play an important role and are central to Marxist thinking. This has a number of benefits in that it links the major social institutions and highlights the importance of economics within society.

The critics state that this theory gives little freedom to individuals. The emphasis is on conflict. Yet not every society is in conflict all the time. As Marxism considers that conflict is normal, it comes under criticism for this. Marxism also omits gender and ethnic inequality.

Feminism

Feminism examines social experiences from the viewpoint of women. Generally feminism provides a critique of other theories which, it considers, look at society only from the viewpoint of males and make women invisible within society.

Feminism has two main roles:

● To redress the balance and examine society from a female point of view. For example, how women's opportunities are restricted in society.
● To explore women's lives, often neglected by sociological studies.

There are also different types of feminism which look at specific aspects of women in society.

KEY CONCEPTS

Patriarchy is a form of society or social system in which men are seen as being in authority. Power is passed from father to son.

Black:
grew from concerns that black women had been ignored by white feminists

Liberal:
looks at legal restrictions on women in society

Feminism

Marxist:
see feminism as a result of class inequality

Radical:
this theory emphasises the oppressive nature of patriarchy

Feminism believes that gender inequality in society is not natural or functional and is a result of patriarchy. This gives an imbalance of power which is expressed publicly, such as woman being exploited in the economic market, and privately, such as woman being the victims of violence.

Interactionism

The key concept here is the self and how we perceive ourselves in the social world. The emphasis is on the thoughts and actions of individuals. Society is the result of these interactions. As a consequence meaning is placed on society through the interactions people have with each other. Labelling is often used as a control method by those in authority.

Interactionism recognises that individuals are not just passive but have a role within society, but fails to acknowledge why some groups have the power to label others or put constraints on individuals.

New Right

This theory was influential in shaping social and economic policies in the 1980s and 1990s. It introduced market principles into society, especially in areas of public life. It considers that the free market produces wealth and freedom. It also considers that traditional values (such as the family, education and nationalism) are being threatened.

However, this theory has been criticised for destroying community due to its emphasis on market principles.

Post-modernism

> **KEY CONCEPTS**
>
> **Modern society means the industrial world.**

Post-modernism stresses the uncertain natures of societies. Modernism is considered to be a time when study of the world was scientific and traditional. Post-modernism believes that we have moved on from this and can point to various aspects of changes in society, such as shifts in work patterns. Post-modernism looks at a range of theories and considers that they all have a part in and something to say about society.

However, post-modernism has been criticised for not taking into account the role of individuals or the relations between social institutions. Some sociologists also disagree that we are living in a post-modern society.

> **Activity 3**
>
> Linking to P1.
> How would each of these theories view the social structures of society?

Collectivism

Collectivism is a set of political beliefs. This stresses the importance of a collective society. There is an emphasis on group as opposed to individual goals. Therefore each individual has a responsibility to each other individual. There is an emphasis on the government's provision of welfare as opposed to private organisations providing it. Welfare services are universal and as they are provided by the government, individuals within a society can expect their government to provide for them.

2 Apply sociological approaches to health and social care

The sociological perspectives above can be applied to concepts of health and ill health.

Functionalism

This looks at the relationship between the sick person and society as a whole. Medicine serves the wellbeing of society as a whole and the public are protected from people who want to abuse the system. This is mainly through professionals in medicine acting as 'gate keepers'. This also allows those who are legitimately sick to withdraw from society.

Marxism

This approach considers the interests of the capitalist ruling classes. Health is believed to be an individual problem rather than a problem for society. Health is necessary to maintain a healthy workforce and therefore the profits of the ruling classes.

Feminism

Feminists look at how men dominate aspects of health and illness. Feminism considers that medicine is a way of controlling women, as some aspects of health that were once considered to be a normal part of life are now thought of as medical conditions. Feminists also argue that women within health and social care play what are perceived to be lesser roles.

Interactionism

This looks at social interaction in everyday life and the meanings people give to their social experiences. An interactionist looks at health and the meaning, impact and consequences that illness can have in people's lives.

Activity 4

Linking to P2/M1.
Which of these approaches to health do you think are the most useful? What are some of the criticisms of these?

Understanding different concepts of health and ill health

Health can be defined in different ways. The definition of health will have implications for treating ill health and promoting health. It can be considered as:

- negative – defining health in a negative way is to look at health as the absence of any physical illness or disease. As the emphasis is on the physical symptoms it means that the person has done nothing to improve their health
- positive – defining health in a positive way is to look at health by saying a person achieves a healthy state through their own contribution to wellbeing
- holistic – looks at treating the whole person rather than specific parts or aspects

The World Health Organisation offered the following definition in 1946: 'Health is a state of complete physical, mental and social wellbeing and not merely the absence of disease or infirmity.'

Models of health

Health can be defined and considered in two ways. These are the biomedical and sociomedical models.

Biomedical model

The emphasis here is on the treating of ill health. The human body is a fixable machine. If this malfunctions then health is lost. Ill health is a temporary state and can therefore be fixed. It is treated after symptoms appear.

Ill health is down to specific diseases. These illnesses can be diagnosed by a health professional. This professional is the only person with the expertise to tell whether a person is sick or healthy. Disease has a cause and is treated at an individual level. Illness is a temporary state and is treated in a professional place. This illness occurs naturally and independently of social behaviour or social influences. Health is defined in a negative way and diagnosed through procedures and tests.

However, there are many diseases that the medical profession cannot treat. There may also be other explanations for why there has been a decline in the death rate (these include environmental health).

Sociomedical model

Some sociologists look at the sociomedical model. This places concepts of disease and illness within the way society defines health and illness. It is therefore socially rather than biologically constructed. The social model considers that the medical profession is dominant within society and wants to remain dominant. Therefore it constructs the concept of disease and illness. In order to define illness it is necessary to understand the social context of the illness.

The social model emphasises the importance of factors such as lifestyle, poverty, education, housing and social support.

Activity 5

Linking to P3, M2, D1.
Which explanation do you find most convincing? Discuss this with other people in the class. What are some of the advantages and disadvantages of the two models?

KEY CONCEPTS

To understand society and health and wellbeing, it is necessary to define key terms:

- **illness**: this is considered a subjective feeling that patients have or they may feel unwell although disease is not present

- **disability**: this is a restriction or lack of ability to perform physical or mental functions. Disability can also be defined in medical and social ways

- **iatrogenesis** is doctor-induced illness and disability

- **medicalised** means that problems are seen as being suitable for medical intervention

Iatrogenesis

Illich (1990) looked at the detrimental effects of medicine and considered that these go beyond direct clinical harm. He believed that medicine is trying to play God and, as such, experiences that were once seen as normal have now been medicalised (i.e. categorised as disorders that require medical attention).

Illich considered three types of iatrogenesis:

CLINICAL	SOCIAL	CULTURAL
Harm done due to wrong diagnosis or treatment	Doctors have more control over people's lives (see medicalisation)	A shift in thinking which means that people no longer deal with pain, sickness and death

Activity 6

Thalidomide was prescribed in the 1960s for pregnant women to overcome morning sickness. The consequences were unknown at the time, but the drug left children with severe malformities.

Many children are now being prescribed Ritalin to combat hyperactivity. ADHD (Attention-deficit hyperactivity disorder) and ADD (Attention deficit disorder) are relatively new concepts. There are some people who consider that Ritalin is unnecessary and that other strategies should be employed, such as counselling. Research Thalidomide–related malformities, ADHD and ADD and decide whether they fit into iatrogenesis.

Activity 7

What are your workplace policy and procedures on illness? Do any of these reflect the sick role?

The sick role

In Western societies we expect people to conform to a sick role. Talcot Parsons suggests that having a sick role allows the sick person to withdraw from or suspend their usual roles and obligations, for example work. This means that if a person is sick they are not held responsible for their condition. As a deterrent the sick person is supposed to find the state of being sick undesirable. It therefore places obligation on the sick person to get better by using available health care resources.

This explanation helps us to understand how society expects people to behave when they are ill.

However, it is not so helpful if sociologists want to look at how people experience illness as it looks only at the response to it. In addition, people do not have equal access to the sick role. Some people do not have the option of withdrawing from society. This explanation includes people who will not accept the sick role due to their medical condition. This may include people with mental disorders.

The clinical iceberg

Epsom (1978) carried out a study of health of adults using a mobile clinic. He found that some patients had major diseases such as cancer. These diseases had not been detected by their general practitioner. The clinical iceberg describes the fact that the majority of symptoms are ignored or left untreated.

Understanding patterns and trends in health and Illness

Linking to P5, M3, D2.

There are many ways in which sociologists can measure patterns and trends in health and illness. Each of these reveals different aspects of health and illness.

Morbidity rates

Morbidity looks at sickness rates, whether temporary (acute), long term (chronic) or without cure (terminal). It can be measured through GP sick notes, hospital records or prescriptions dispensed. Some diseases and illnesses are notifiable under legislation. (A notifiable disease is a disease which is recorded and analysed and if necessary public health action is taken. Doctors will report incidences of these diseases to the local authority. Examples include tuberculosis and meningitis.) This could also be a measure of morbidity and may provide information on disease incidence and prevalence. Morbidity will look at the frequency of diseases within population groups.

The advantage of these statistics is that they are reliable. However, a large number of people who are ill do not visit health care professionals. These people are therefore not taken into account when statistics are examined. A patient may also visit the doctor on several occasions for the same symptoms. There is no real way of filtering these out and therefore this may distort the statistics.

Mortality rates

The mortality rate refers to the number of people dying within a particular period per 100,000 of a population.

The standard mortality rate (SMR) assumes the average risk of death for those aged 16–65 years to be 100. Social groups with an SMR of 100+ have a higher risk of an early death. The advantage of mortality rates is that they are objective. They can also give scope for comparing countries. However, a mortality rate does not reflect the quality of life the person has. For health and social care professionals this would be an important consideration.

Activity 8

Look up the mortality rates for two countries. What do you think might be some of the explanations for the differences (if any) between the two?

Health surveillance

This measures the frequency of health and illness revealed by screening results. It can predict symptoms and illness that may occur. However, health professionals are not able to screen for all illness, which means that this way of measuring health and illness is not a true representation. In addition, not everyone who is entitled to screening procedures will use them.

Activity 9

Why do people not use available health screening? How as health and social care professionals can we encourage people to access screening?

Patterns and trends of health and illness

Although there are problems in measuring health, certain patterns and trends can be identified within different groups.

Age

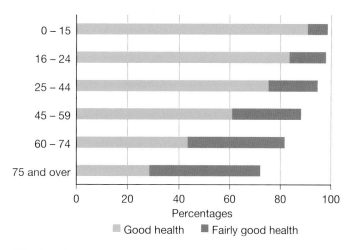

Status of health at various ages
Source: National Statistics – www.statistics.gov.uk

There are differences in illness reported according to age and general health. Children under 16 were reported as having the best health. The least healthy were older people over 75 years.

Activity 10

Research the illnesses associated with age. Which are more common in younger people and which in older people? Why do you think this may be the case?

Gender

There are differences in life expectancy and certain illnesses between the genders. Life expectancy has improved for both genders. However, statistics show that causes of illness and death differ between the genders. Social Trends states: 'In 2002 disability-free life expectancy at birth was 63.0 years for females and 60.9 years for males. However, while women can expect to live longer than men they are also more likely to spend more years in poor health or with a disability.'

Social class

Differences in social class are some of the key highlighted issues within the Black Report and a key recommendation of the Acheson Report. The Black Report was published by the Department of Health and Social Security in 1980. The report was the result of a committee chaired by Sir Douglas Black looking into health inequalities. The committee found that there were marked and widespread health inequalities, even though the general health of the population had improved. The Acheson Report was a report on health inequalities published by the Department of Health in 1998. It looked into health inequalities and suggested areas for policy development. It highlighted a range of areas where health inequalities could be reduced. These included education, with more funding for schools (because disadvantaged children achieve less well at school), and restrictions on smoking (because the poorer you are, the more likely you are to smoke).

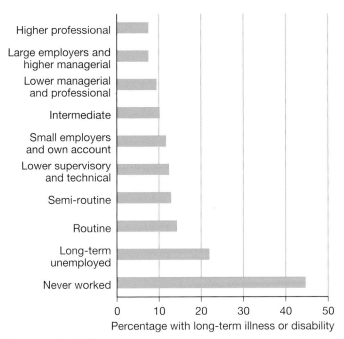

Long-term illness or disability
Source: National Statistics – www.statistics.gov.uk

Statistics from the National Statistics Online (2001) show that people not in employment have higher levels of long-term illness or disability.

Ethnicity

There are also inequalities within health and ethnicity. Statistics show that limiting long-term illness is higher in Pakistani and Bangladeshi people.

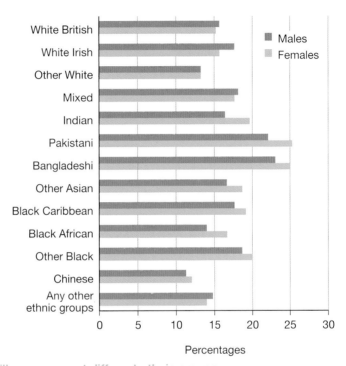

Long-term illness amongst different ethnic groups
Source: National Statistics – www.statistics.gov.uk

Locality

Within the UK there are differences in health and illness reported by locality. Statistics show that the lowest life expectancies are in the North East and in the North West, while the highest life expectancies are in the South East, South West and East of England.

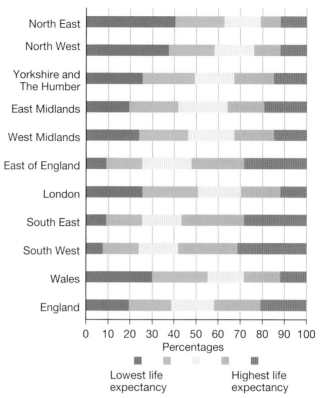

Life expectancies by region
Source: National Statistics – www.statistics.gov.uk

Sociological explanations for illness

Sociologists have looked at explanations for these variations in health and illness.

Artefact

This explanation looks at the relationship between social variables and health. It states that the statistical evidence is false and therefore invalid. Health and inequality is a statistical fiction which is created by the way in which data are gathered and analysed.

Health inequalities feature predominantly within statistics and this cannot be explained solely by false data and methods of analysis.

Natural/social selection

This explanation considers that health inequality is the result of genetic or biological factors. Inequalities are seen as beneficial to society. It is health that causes a person to be in a certain class, not class that causes a person to be in a certain state of health. If a person is disabled or has a chronic illness they will not be able to work and therefore will remain in a lower social class.

However, this has been heavily criticised for being too fatalistic. There is a consensus that health and class inequality are related. Statistics show that people in poor health are more likely to be in lower-paid positions.

Behavioural

Variations in health status are attributable to different norms, values and attitudes. People make a lifestyle choice, such as poor diet or smoking, thus leading to poorer health.

To overcome health inequalities it is necessary to resocialise people through education and the media. If messages are ignored, people have only themselves to blame.

Structural

This explanation considers that people have unequal access to resources owing to differing material and environmental circumstances. It is social structures that determine lifestyle and influence health.

The structural approach considers that people in lower classes have limited choices as a consequence of their poverty. The nature of their working and domestic lives leads to poor health. This theory absolves people of any responsibility for their health status.

Each of these theories can be applied to the inequalities in gender, social class and ethnicity that have been displayed in the statistics.

Sociological explanations for health inequalities

	ARTEFACT	NATURAL/ SOCIAL SELECTION	BEHAVIOURAL/ CULTURAL	MATERIALIST/ STRUCTURALIST
Social class	Even though statistics show a relationship between class and health, this may be due to the way in which the data are collected or the way in which class is defined. It does not automatically mean that class and ill health are linked.	Ill health causes a person to be in a specific class. Those that are fitter will be able to obtain better jobs.	The differences are related to the lifestyle choices made by people in specific classes.	Ill health in the lower classes is due to social structures. People are ill due to an unequal society.

	ARTEFACT	NATURAL/ SOCIAL SELECTION	BEHAVIOURAL/ CULTURAL	MATERIALIST/ STRUCTURALIST
Gender	Inequalities exist due to the way in which data are collected. For example, more women than men seek advice as men are conditioned to have a 'stiff upper lip'.	Women are seen as weaker. Men and women are more likely to be subject to different types of illness.	This explanation relates to the activities that men and women may become involved in. Men, for example, may be more likely to partake in 'risky' activities. They may also be more likely to smoke and drink excessively, which has its own set of health risks.	This explanation considers that there is a link between social inequalities of gender and poor health.
Ethnicity	Inequalities exist due to the way in which data are collected and interpreted.	The differences exist due to the various ethnic groups being more vulnerable to different types of illness or disease. This includes sickle cell disease.	This considers that those differences from ethnic minorities may be due to the unhealthy behaviour of people from these groups.	This explanation considers that those from ethnic minority groups are more likely to be discriminated against or have poorer life chances.

How useful is this explanation?

Each explanation provides solutions to inequality.

- *Artefact.* As this explanation considers that inequality is due to the way in which statistics are gathered, no action is necessary – just an improvement in the way in which statistics are collected! However, this does not actually explain the differences in mortality rates between the variables.
- *Natural/social selection.* The solution to health inequality is to take no action. As inequality is seen as beneficial, any interference would be dangerous. This does, however, lead to a deterministic acceptance of ill health.
- *Behavioural.* The solution to health inequality according to this approach is to resocialise people and educate them into improving their health. However, this fails to consider the many other factors that impact upon a person's health.
- *Structural.* The solution for this explanation is to redistribute resources which will impact positively upon the underlying causes. The Black Report highlighted this explanation as the most important. However, this does not take into account any individual responsibility and clears individuals from blame for their own ill health.

Activity 11

Linking to M3, D2. Which explanation do you think is the most useful? Why?

SUMMARY

● Sociology is the study of society. There are various perspectives and theories which provide different ways of looking at society.

● There are variations in morbidity and mortality in the UK. This may be on the basis of gender, age, ethnicity or locality.

● There are health inequalities within society and sociologists can provide some explanation for these.

Grading grid

In order to pass this unit, the evidence that the learner presents for assessment needs to demonstrate that they can meet all of the learning outcomes for the unit. The criteria for a pass grade describe the level of achievement required to pass this unit.

GRADING CRITERIA

TO ACHIEVE A PASS GRADE THE EVIDENCE MUST SHOW THAT THE LEARNER IS ABLE TO:	TO ACHIEVE A MERIT GRADE THE EVIDENCE MUST SHOW THAT, IN ADDITION TO THE PASS CRITERIA, THE LEARNER IS ABLE TO:	TO ACHIEVE A DISTINCTION GRADE THE EVIDENCE MUST SHOW THAT, IN ADDITION TO THE PASS AND MERIT CRITERIA, THE LEARNER IS ABLE TO:
P1 use sociological terminology to describe the principal sociological perspectives		
P2 describe different concepts of health	M1 use two sociological perspectives to explain different concepts of health	
P3 describe the biomedical and sociomedical models of health	M2 explain the biomedical and socio-medical models of health	D1 evaluate the biomedical and sociomedical models of health
P4 describe different concepts of ill health	M3 use sociological explanations for health inequalities to explain the patterns and trends of health and illness in three different social groups.	D2 evaluate the four sociological explanations for health inequalities in terms of explaining the patterns and trends of health and illness in three different social groups.
P5 compare patterns and trends of health and illness in three different social groups.		

Psychological Perspectives for Health and Social Care

8

This unit provides an introduction to different psychological perspectives and shows how these perspectives can be used in health and social care.

Learning Outcomes

On completion of this unit you should be able to:

1 Understand psychological approaches to study
2 Apply psychological approaches to health and social care

Psychology was studied in Ancient Greece over 2000 years ago. The Ancient Greek word 'psyche' meant 'mind' or 'soul'. Anything that ends in 'ology' refers to the study of a subject, so 'psychology' refers to the study of mental processes and behaviour. Animal psychology is the study of animal behaviour. Child psychology is the study of child behaviour. When you study this unit, you are learning about a subject that has fascinated people for thousands of years: why do we behave the way we do?

The Acropolis in Athens dates from the time of Ancient Greece

1 Understand psychological approaches to study
2 Apply psychological approaches to health and social care

In this section we will look at six major perspectives or theories of psychology. These are outlined in the diagram below.

Did you know?

Although there are several psychological perspectives, many psychologists now think that there is no one correct perspective, but that a combination of views may best explain behaviour.

Ivan Pavlov

The behaviourist perspective

Behaviourists believed there is a scientific explanation for behaviour. They used methods such as scientific experiment and observation of results to explain how people behaved.

Two of the main theorists were Ivan Pavlov and B. F. Skinner.

Ivan Pavlov studied dogs and found that when a bell was rung at feeding time, the dogs salivated. Gradually he withdrew the food but rang the bell and noticed that the dogs still salivated. He called this classical conditioning. The dogs associated the sound of the bell with food and were conditioned to respond to the bell.

Babies who are bottle fed often know when it is milk time because they recognise the signs of a parent getting the bottle ready. They may start salivating too. Sometimes if the parent is getting the bottle ready for later in the day, the baby gets confused and wonders where the milk is.

B. F. Skinner

B. F. Skinner (1904–1990) researched operant conditioning. This is where conditioning is used to modify behaviour. Key terms are:

- reinforcement – where a consequence causes behaviour to occur more often. A child who is praised for picking up his toys will do so again in the hope of being praised again
- punishment – causes behaviour to occur less often, so a young person who is caught shoplifting and charged with the offence will think carefully before shoplifting again
- extinction – a term to describe no consequence following a response. Experienced parents may use this with a toddler to reduce pester power in the supermarket. If the parent does not respond to the child's demands, the child gets bored and stops asking.

Skinner used positive reinforcement and negative reinforcement with rats. He also used positive punishment and negative punishment. See the table below for an explanation.

	POSITIVE	NEGATIVE
Reinforcement	Desired behaviour gets a positive reward. Skinner used rats. When rats pressed a lever, they got a reward of sugar	Desired behaviour gets the removal of discomfort. Skinner sounded a loud noise in the rat's cage. When the rat pressed the lever, the noise stopped
Punishment	Undesirable behaviour gets an unpleasant response, so a rat showing undesirable behaviour may get a mild electric shock. A child who runs into the road may get shouted at	Undesirable behaviour results in the removal of something pleasurable, so a rat showing undesirable behaviour may have food withdrawn. A child who hits another child may have a toy taken away

Skinner believed that behaviour could be changed or modified, but he did not believe that punishment worked. He reasoned that if punishment worked, people would not go back into prison.

Skinner believed in positive reinforcement, rewarding the desired behaviour. Some teachers and social workers use this technique to manage behaviour in young people. Parents find this method effective too.

Activity 1

For P1.
What do you think – which works best, punishment or praise?
Work in pairs and take one view each. Prepare your side of the debate, with examples from placement to support your view.
You may use the material above to help you meet P1. Describe the application of behaviourist perspectives in health and social care.

Social learning

Social learning means learning from others. The desired behaviour is observed, then modelled symbolically, in play, then acted out for real. Words, images and an identity help fix the behaviour, so in the example below, boys identify with the Johnson Crew or the Burger Bar Boys. As young children they may play at shooting, but as they grow up they join the gang and use guns for real.

People are more likely to adopt a modelled behaviour if it results in outcomes they value. Being a member of a gang gives status and protection. It is more probable that they will join a gang if members are similar to themselves. An admired older brother is a role model for younger brothers to follow. If the older brother joins a gang, the younger ones may join too.

Case Study: HomeBoys, the Birmingham Gang War and the New Year's Eve Murders

Amardeep Bassey (2006) investigated Birmingham gang culture.

At a New Year party in 2003, two teenage girls were cut down in a hail of machine gun fire. The brutal killings brought the Birmingham gang war to national attention. Amardeep Bassey was the first to identify the rival gangs – the Johnson Crew and the Burger Bar Boys – and detail their feud.

In *HomeBoys* he traces their roots back to the mid-1980s, when groups of young black men banded together to counter threats to their community from the Far Right. They evolved into criminal street gangs that could call on almost 300 street soldiers. The Johnson Crew's territory was Aston and Nechells. The Burger Bar Boys claimed Handsworth – scene of the 1985 riots – Lozells and Perry Bar. From the beginning they were at war, fuelled by the growing market for crack. They forged links with gangs in Manchester and London and acquired a fearsome array of weaponry.

Source: www.amazon.co.uk

Remember

Telling yourself you are good at something may help you become good at it! This is the basis of many courses in self-improvement.

Activity 2

Towards P2.
Explain the value of the social learning approach to health and social care service provision. Use examples from your placement.

Social learning may be positive too. Children learn to respect older people by modelling the behaviour of others around them, so in cultures where age is respected, young people will model the behaviour of their elders and learn to respect them. Children learn good manners from their parents and from those they admire.

Another type of social learning is the self-fulfilling prophecy. This is a prediction that originally is false but becomes true. Robert King Merton first used the term. In a famous educational experiment conducted by Meichenbaum (1969), a teacher was told that in the new class, certain students had high academic potential. In fact this was not true at the start of the experiment, but at the end, when performance was measured, the students labelled as potentially better had in fact become better performers. This was due to the teacher's expectations of them.

Role theory implies that if we know the role expectations for a specified position much of the behaviour of the person in that role can be predicted. We may expect a teacher to be fair and to explain a subject. We do not expect a teacher to provide us with clothes or bus fare because that is not part of a teacher's role.

Albert Bandura's social learning theory says human behaviour is a result of continuous interaction between cognitive, behavioural and environmental influences. The diagram below may help you understand this.

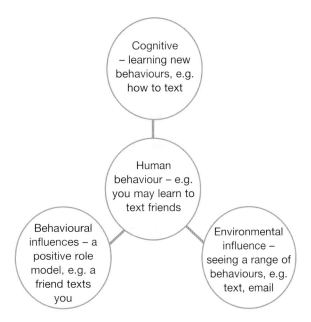

The stages of social learning are:

1   attention, recognising a behaviour, for example doing a creative activity at placement. First you watch someone else
2   retention, including rehearsal of the behaviour. You may imagine what you would say or do in that situation
3   motor reproduction, so you try it out and use self-observation and feedback to check how it went
4   motivation – you may be praised by your tutor for getting involved, or you feel a sense of achievement in overcoming your nerves

The psychodynamic perspective

The psychodynamic perspective emphasises the importance of the unconscious mind and of early experiences. Sigmund Freud (1856–1939) developed the psychodynamic school of psychology. His theory states that there are three parts to our mind:

- the 'id' (fully unconscious) contains drives and basic instincts. A baby passes urine without thinking about it
- the 'ego' (mostly conscious) deals with external reality so the child learns the rules of society, for example to use the toilet
- the 'super ego' (partly conscious) is the conscience or the internal moral judge, so a child who knows where the toilet is and how to use it but has an 'accident' may feel ashamed

You may be able to think of a case study from placement which involves a similar situation.

Freud also said that early experiences shape us. He described the following stages of development:

- *Oral* (0–18 months). In this stage the baby puts everything to the mouth.
- *Anal* (18 months–3½ years). During this phase the child learns to control bowels and gains pleasure from this.
- *Phallic* (3½–6 years). In this phase, children are working out what it means to be a girl or boy. Freud said that children fall in love with the parent of the opposite sex. Boys love their mothers most at this stage – the Oedipus complex, while girls love their fathers – the Electra complex.
- *Latency* (6 years–puberty). This is a period of calm in a child's life.
- *Genital* (puberty–adulthood). This is a period of creativity when work and love are balanced. The person is psychologically well adjusted and balanced. The child grows into the adult and is no longer 'in love' with the opposite-sex parent but may identify with their values, so a girl who loved her father because he was kind will, as an adult, adopt this as her own value and will try to be kind.

If a person does not work through a stage, they may revert to that stage when stressed. In health and care situations you may see service users who revert to a previous stage of behaviour when they are upset, so an adult may behave childishly.

Freud believed that personality is formed by the age of five, whereas Erik Erikson believed that changes happen throughout life. Erikson's theory of life stages is widely used in health and social care. This is a psychodynamic theory which looks at how emotional and motivational forces affect behaviour. Erikson described eight stages that humans pass through. These are explained in the table on the next page.

STAGE	AGE	WHAT HAPPENS
Trust vs. Mistrust	birth to 1 year	The baby learns to trust the world about them if someone responds to their cry. If the child is neglected, the child will be frustrated, withdrawn, suspicious, and will lack self-confidence.
Autonomy vs. Shame and Doubt	2–3 years	The child needs a supportive atmosphere so it can develop a sense of self-control without a loss of self-esteem. If a child does not trust the world, or is labelled as naughty, they will experience shame and doubt. A child opens a cupboard and pulls out glasses. A carer who says the child is naughty will instil shame and doubt. A carer who encourages exploration also encourages independence and autonomy. Of course the carer must make sure the environment is safe for the child by removing breakable objects.
Initiative vs. Guilt	4–5 years	The child develops a sense of responsibility which increases initiative during this period. If the child is made to feel too anxious, they will feel guilty.
Industry vs. Inferiority	6 years– puberty	The child starts school and learns about the world through books and technology. The child learns from every aspect of the environment and is eager to learn. Success and mastery bring a feeling of achievement and encourage further industry. Failure at this stage makes them feel inferior.
Identity vs. Role confusion	adolescence	The child emerges as an adolescent and forges a new identity or remains confused about their role, sometimes acting childishly.
Intimacy vs. Isolation	young adulthood	The young person either remains isolated or enters a close and intimate relationship.
Generativity vs. Stagnation	adulthood	This creative and nurturing phase encourages the younger generation in developing and leading useful lives too. An unfulfilled life is stagnant.
Integrity vs. Despair	older age	This is when the individual looks back and evaluates their life. Some feel they have had a good life and have few regrets. They experience integrity. Some people feel bitter and betrayed by lack of life chances. They are full of regrets and may despair.

Erikson's eight stages

Activity 3

For P3.

Describe the application of psychodynamic perspectives in health and social care. Use a case study from your placement if possible, otherwise use a case study of someone you know.

- Which Erikson life stage do you think they are in? Explain your answer.
- What stages have they already been through and how do you think they reacted?
- Using the same case study, which aspect of their personality dominates – the id, the ego or the superego? Explain your answer.

The humanistic perspective

The humanistic perspective includes theories by Maslow and Rogers. Abraham Maslow published *A Theory of Human Motivation* in 1943, after studying high achievers. His theory states that there are five levels of need and they are hierarchical, that is, one must be fulfilled before the next one can be. The needs are usually represented in a triangle.

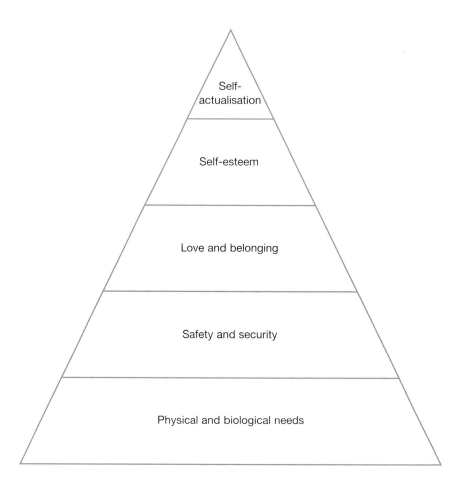

The top level of needs is a growth need. The bottom four needs are deficiency needs. Only when all the deficiency needs are met can an individual self-actualise, be spontaneous and confident in who they are and be truly creative.

Some people achieve self-actualisation later in life. Some people never achieve this stage, while others may achieve it early. A person may be self-actualising, but if they are suddenly plunged into a situation where they are in danger, with no food or water, they can no longer self-actualise but must focus on basic needs.

The following case studies are two examples of Maslow's theory applied to health and social care.

Case Studies

A person may be settled, able to meet their basic needs and be self-actualising, but then is made redundant. Unable to manage financially, they cannot pay their mortgage and may become homeless. From being a confident person achieving all they want to achieve, they now have to think about their basic needs, not knowing whether they will eat that day.

A retired 80-year-old music teacher lives alone but has a circle of friends and likes to holiday abroad. Each year she visits a new country and learns some of the language before she goes, researching it on the internet first. One icy day she slips and breaks her leg. She is admitted to hospital. When she is ready for discharge, she is unable to climb the steps to her upstairs bathroom so the decision is made that she has to stay in residential care. In the care home, she is no longer independent, has nothing to read and is unable to pursue her hobbies. She is dependent on others for her food, warmth and even a drink of water.

Self-concept

Self-concept is a person's knowledge and understanding of his or her self. Self-concept has physical, psychological and social aspects, which can be influenced by the individual's attitudes, habits and beliefs. These form self-image and self-esteem.

Social psychologist Erich Fromm (1900–1980) described self-concept as 'life being aware of itself'.

A baby is not born with a self-concept. The child gradually learns who he or she is and where they fit in the family. Self-concept is learned. A child may be physically active, psychologically confident and socially confident. These aspects are organised by the child into a self-concept. As the child grows, self-concept changes. A confident toddler may become a shy teenager. A shy teenager may later become a confident adult. Self-concept is learned, organised and dynamic. Self-concept and self-esteem are closely linked. A person who feels good about themselves may also have high self-esteem.

Carl Ransom Rogers (1902–1987) worked with Abraham Maslow and founded the humanist approach to psychology. He developed the idea of a person-centred approach to psychotherapy. The person or client is the focus, not the therapist. In *On Becoming a Person: A therapist's view of psychotherapy* (1961), he said: 'It is the client who knows what hurts, what directions to go, what problems are crucial, what experiences have been deeply buried.'

A key factor in the development of personality is whether a child is raised with unconditional positive regard. 'Unconditional positive regard' means that the child is accepted for itself, with no conditions attached. A child who is loved in this way will develop freely and self-actualise. A child who is told 'we won't love you if …' receives conditional regard and is scared to experiment or be creative in case affection is withdrawn.

Rogers believed that self-actualisation was not just about happiness but about experiencing a rich and full life where the individual is not afraid to live and may experience pain as well as happiness.

According to Rogers, a fully functioning person is open rather than defensive, lives each moment fully rather than thinking about what comes next, trusts their own judgement of a situation, makes choices and takes responsibility for their behaviour. The fully functioning person is creative and reliable. They experience the good life which, according to Rogers, 'involves the courage to be. It means launching oneself fully into the stream of life' (Rogers, 1961).

Activity 4

Towards P4.
Describe the value of the humanistic approach to health and social care service provision.
Give an example from your placement where Maslow's hierarchy of needs may be useful in understanding a service user's situation.
How could knowledge of Carl Roger's person-centred approach be used in health and social care?

Cognitive perspective/information processing

Jean Piaget (1896–1980) described four stages of development:

- Sensori-motor stage: from birth to age 2 years where children experience the world through movement and through their senses. They learn that objects covered over by a blanket do not disappear.
- Pre-operational stage: from ages 2 to 7 where children develop motor skills such as hopping, skipping and writing.
- Concrete operational stage: from ages 7 to 11 where children begin to think logically about concrete events and can see that 12 sweets shared between four children gives three sweets each.
- Formal operational stage: after age 11 children can reason that 13 sweets shared between four children will leave one sweet remaining. They will not need to physically have the sweets to work through the problem. They use abstract reasoning.

Some people with learning difficulties may be at a different stage even though by chronological age they are considered adult.

Activity 5

Mary is 30 years old and has learning difficulties. She is putting out the biscuits for coffee. There are five people for coffee and they need two biscuits each. She needs to put two biscuits on each plate, then count them all to find out how many biscuits she used. Which stage do you think she is at according to Piaget's theory? Did you recognise the concrete operational stage?

George Kelly's personal construct theory (PCT) is widely used in education and management to help make sense of how an individual views the world. The individual interprets the world around them by seeing patterns of events, similarities and contrasts. They refine these constructs in the light of further events.

Core constructs govern the processes by which people maintain their identities. These super-ordinate constructs tend to be more fixed and the individual may be reluctant to change these ideas, for example a person may see themselves as unattractive even though others do not.

An individual may not be aware of their personal constructs. Kelly devised a 'role construct repertory test' to help people identify some of their personal constructs. Here is an example of how it works:

- Compare and contrast your mother, your father, yourself.
- How are two of them the same?
- How do two of them differ?

The individual may say that they are like their mother and have a trusting nature, but father is not as trusting as mother. This then identifies that 'trusting' is one of the individual's core constructs.

These results can be noted on a repertory grid, such as the one below.

| CONSTRUCT | ELEMENTS | | | | CONSTRUCT |
	MOTHER	FATHER	SELF	BEST FRIEND	
trusting	1	7	1	5	suspicious
emotional					logical
attractive					unattractive
popular					unpopular

Groups of three are presented each time, so the individual can say how they are like someone and how they differ from someone. They can then say how each element would score on a rating of 1 to 7, with 1 being the most. A trusting mother would score 1. A suspicious father would score 7. The individual may score themselves as being as trusting as their mother. They may say their best friend is more trusting than their father but not as trusting as their mother.

Repertory grids can be complicated and statistical packages may be used to analyse the more complicated ones. (*Source*: www.pcp-net.org/encyclopaedia)

A resident in a care home was staring out of the window. The sun was shining, birds were singing and the first flowers of spring were in bloom, but the service user saw only a blank emptiness stretching ahead.

How could Kelly's personal construct theory be used to help them?

First, it is important for carers to be aware of their limitations. Unless a person is employed as a trained and qualified counsellor, they should not attempt to counsel a service user. Yet carers do interact with service users and want to help.

Sitting with a service user or resident, just being with them if they do not want to talk, can be supportive. A service user who is emotionally upset may want to talk and they may need someone to listen.

A depressed individual may need more specialist help, but getting them to talk may be a way of establishing contact and giving support. They may offer their view of how they are 'as unlucky as my mother in picking men'. This tells the skilled helper that the individual's view of themselves is as unlucky. They may say that they 'get walked over just like their dad' or 'I'm not like my sister who is a money-grabbing career woman with no time for her family'. The service user is showing their values in the way they talk about others.

A service user with depression may have a view of themselves or the world which others do not recognise. The service user seeing a blank emptiness is not seeing the flowers that others see. Sometimes a carer can point out the positive aspects of a situation and help the service user reframe their view of life. Sometimes this is a role for a skilled counsellor.

Activity 6

For P5.
Explain the value of the cognitive perspective in supporting individuals. You may wish to give an example using Piaget's cognitive development theory applied to a case study from placement.

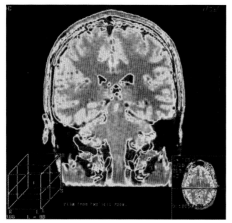
MRI scans can identify regions of high brain activity

Biological perspective

Maturational theory states that development depends on maturation, especially of the nervous system. Psychologist and paediatrician Arnold L. Gesell said that behaviour seems to follow a set developmental pattern, for example there is a critical period when humans learn language. This cannot happen until the nerve pathways in the brain have developed enough for the baby to distinguish sounds. Similarly, walking happens only when the child develops control of the muscles in the legs and back. Reading happens only after a child has learned to focus and control eye movements.

Recent research on the development of teenage brains has provided evidence to support the view that teenagers cannot help their emotional outbursts. The adolescent brain undergoes massive changes and does not reach maturity until 20 or 30 years old. See http://news.bbc.co.uk/1/hi/sci/tech/5327550.stm for more about this research.

Activity 7

Read about the study into teenage brain development at http://news.bbc.co.uk/1/hi/sci/tech/5327550.stm. According to this research, why is it unreasonable to ask a teenager to think about other people's feelings?

Although Gesell believed in the importance of genetic influences on behaviour, he was also aware that nurture or upbringing has an effect on how children develop.

Several twin studies have been carried out to try to find out how much of behaviour is due to genes and how much is due to nurture. Monozygotic (MZ, identical) twins share all of their genes, while dizygotic (DZ, fraternal) twins share only half of their genes. Therefore identical twins should be more alike than fraternal twins. One famous study of twins separated at birth suggests a strong link between genes and behaviour.

Thomas J. Bouchard is director of the Minnesota Center for Twin and Adoption Research, University of Minnesota. In 1979, Bouchard came across a pair of twins, Jim Springer and Jim Lewis, who, separated from birth, were reunited at the age of 39. 'The twins,' Bouchard later wrote, 'were found to have married women named Linda, divorced, and married the second time to women named Betty. One named his son James Allan, the other named his son James Alan, and both named their pet dogs Toy.'

The importance of genetic influences on autism, bipolar disorder and other mental health issues is being researched at the Maudesley hospital in London.

Imbalance

Sometimes endocrine or hormonal imbalance may cause obesity. A low thyroid function rate, polycystic ovaries, or other endocrine problems such as Cushing's syndrome may result in weight gain.

Another biological reason for changes in health and behaviour may be lack of sleep due to disrupted sleep rhythms. Circadian rhythms are our body's natural pattern and are linked to light levels which in turn are linked to hormones. When we work shifts or do not sleep regularly, our circadian rhythm is disturbed. Go to http://news.bbc.co.uk/go/pr/fr/-/1/hi/health/6120546.stm to read about the effects of jetlag on our health.

Activity 8

What effect might shift work have on doctors, nurses and care workers if they do not have enough sleep?

Activity 9

For P6.
Describe the application of biological perspectives in health and social care. How might biological perspectives help in understanding:

● late development in children?
● childhood obesity?
● mood swings of teenagers in care?

SUMMARY

After working through this unit you should be able to:

- describe the application of behaviourist perspectives in health and social care

- explain the value of the social learning approach to health and social care service provision

- describe the application of psychodynamic perspectives in health and social care

- describe the value of the humanistic approach to health and social care service provision

- explain the value of the cognitive perspective in supporting individuals

- describe the application of biological perspectives in health and social care.

Grading grid

In order to pass this unit, the evidence that the learner presents for assessment needs to demonstrate that they can meet all of the learning outcomes for the unit. The criteria for a pass grade describe the level of achievement required to pass this unit.

GRADING CRITERIA

TO ACHIEVE A PASS GRADE THE EVIDENCE MUST SHOW THAT THE LEARNER IS ABLE TO:	TO ACHIEVE A MERIT GRADE THE EVIDENCE MUST SHOW THAT, IN ADDITION TO THE PASS CRITERIA, THE LEARNER IS ABLE TO:	TO ACHIEVE A DISTINCTION GRADE THE EVIDENCE MUST SHOW THAT, IN ADDITION TO THE PASS AND MERIT CRITERIA, THE LEARNER IS ABLE TO:
P1 describe the application of behaviourist perspectives in health and social care		
P2 explain the value of the social learning approach to health and social care service provision		
P3 describe the application of psychodynamic perspectives in health and social care	M1 analyse the contribution of different psychological perspectives to the understanding and management of challenging behaviour	
P4 describe the value of the humanistic approach to health and social care service provision	M2 analyse the contribution of different psychological perspectives to health and social care service provision.	D1 evaluate the roles of different psychological perspectives in health and social care.
P5 explain the value of the cognitive perspective in supporting individuals		
P6 describe the application of biological perspectives in health and social care.		

Useful Websites

Achondroplasia UK: www.achondroplasia.co.uk

Action on Smoking and Health: www.ash.org.uk

Age Concern: www.ageconcern.org.uk

Alcoholics Anonymous: www.alcoholics-anonymous.org.uk

BBC: www.bbc.co.uk

British Association for Counselling and Psychotherapy: www.bacp.co.uk

British Heart Foundation: www.bhf.org.uk

British Red Cross: www.redcross.org.uk

BUPA Care Homes: www.bupacarehomes.co.uk

Care Council for Wales: www.ccwales.org.uk

Carers UK: www.carersuk.org

Clouds: www.actiononaddiction.org.uk

Commission for Racial Equality: www.cre.gov.uk

Commission for Social Care Inspection (CSCI): www.csci.org.uk

Community Care: www.communitycare.co.uk

Community Development: www.cdx.org.uk

Cystic Fibrosis Trust: www.cftrust.org.uk

Department of Health, Social Services and Public Safety, Northern Ireland: www.dhsspsni.gov.uk

Disability Rights Commission: www.drc.org.uk

Downs Syndrome: www.downs-syndrome.org.uk

Equal Opportunities Commission: www.eoc.org.uk

Every Child Matters: www.everychildmatters.gov.uk

Expert Patients Programme: www.worcestershirehealth.nhs.uk/swpct

Feral Children: www.feralchildren.com

Gamblers Anonymous: www.gamblersanonymous.org.uk

General Social Care Council: www.gscc.org.uk

Golden Lane Project: www.glh.org.uk

Great Ape Trust of Iowa: www.greatapetrust.org

Health Protection Agency: www.hpa.org.uk

Health Protection Scotland: www.hps.scot.nhs.uk

HealthScotland: www.healthscotland.com

HM Treasury: www.hm-treasury.gov.uk

Hollyoaks: www.channel4.com/entertainment/tv/microsites/H/hollyoaks

Information Centre for Health and Social Care: www.ic.nhs.uk

Institute of Psychiatry: www.iop.kcl.ac.uk

Joseph Rowntree Foundation: www.jrf.org.uk

Liverpool Mental Health Consortium: www.livementalhealth.org.uk

London South Bank University: www.lsbu.ac.uk

Mind: www.mind.org.uk

National Attention Deficit Disorder Information and Support Service: www.addiss.co.uk

National Audit Office: www.nao.org.uk

National Autistic Society: www.autism.org.uk

National Health Service Give Up Smoking campaigns: www.gosmokefree.co.uk/getunhooked www.gosmokefree.co.uk/onlinematerials/download/index.php

National Institute for Health and Clinical Excellence: www.nice.org.uk

National Public Health Service for Wales: www.wales.nhs.uk

National Statistics Online: www.statistics.gov.uk

New Scientist: www.newscientist.com

NHS Direct: www.nhsdirect.nhs.uk

NHS Heart Improvement Programme: www.heart.nhs.uk

Northern Ireland Social Care Council: www.niscc.info

Nursing Standard: www.nursing-standard.co.uk

Open University: www.open.ac.uk

Pan American Health Organization: www.paho.org

RNIB: www.rnib.org.uk

RNID: www.rnid.org.uk

Road Safety: www.hedgehogs.gov.uk/main/main.html

Roman baths: www.romanbaths.co.uk

Royal College of Psychiatrists: www.rcpsych.ac.uk

Self Harm: www.selfharm.org.uk

Sickle Cell Society: www.sicklecellsociety.org

Social Exclusion Task Force: www.cabinetoffice.gov.uk/
social_exclusion_task_force

Social Exclusion Unit: www.socialexclusion.gov.uk

Social and Spatial Inequalities:
www.sasi.group.shef.ac.uk

Social Trends: ww.statistics.gov.uk/CCI/nugget.asp?
ID=1007&Pos=4&ColRank=2&Rank=224

South Birmingham PCT:
www.southbirminghampct.nhs.uk/_news

Statistics on work injuries:
www.hse.gov.uk/statistics/overall/hssh0506.pdf

Stonewall: www.stonewall.org.uk

Stroke Association: www.stroke.org.uk

The Dostiyo Project:
www.connect2northamptonshire.com

The Drinkaware Trust: www.drinkawaretrust.org.uk

The Guardian: www.guardian.co.uk

The London Bus Theatre:
www.londonbustheatre.co.uk

The Men's Project Northern Ireland:
http://mensproject.org

The Poverty Site: www.poverty.org.uk

The Scottish Executive: www.scotland.gov.uk

The Stanford Prison Experiment: www.prisonexp.org

THINK! Road Safety Website:
www.thinkroadsafety.gov.uk/campaigns/teenagers/t
eenagers.htm

Truancy Sweeps: www.dfes.gov.uk/schoolattendance/
truancysweeps

Victoria Climbie Inquiry: www.victoria-climbie-
inquiry.org.uk

Voluntary Action Camden: www.kingsfund.org.uk/
funding/work_we_have_supported/sexual_health_
1.html

Wikipedia: www.wikipedia.org

World Health Organisation: www.who.int

References

Ainsworth, M.D.S. and Bowlby, J. (1991) 'An Ethological Approach to Personality Development', *American Psychologist*, 46: 331–341.

Alcock, P. (1997) *The Student's Companion to Social Policy*, Blackwell Publishers.

Baillargeon, R. and De Vos, J. (1991) 'Object Permanence in Young Infants: Further Evidence', *Child Development*, 62: 1227–1246.

Barnes, C. (1992) *Disabling Imagery and the Media: An Exploration of the Principles for Media Representations of Disabled People*, Keele University Press.

Bartley, M. (2004) *Health Inequalities – An Introduction to Theories, Concepts and Methods*, Polity Press.

Beck, A.T. (1967) *Depression: Causes and Treatment*, University of Pennsylvania Press.

Bell, J. (1999) *Doing Your Research Project*, Open University Press.

Berkowitz, R. in Gross, R. (2005) *Psychology: The Science of Mind and Behaviour*, Hodder Arnold.

Berthoud, D. (1997) 'Income and Standards of Living' in Modood *et al.*, *Ethnic Minorities in Britain: Diversity and Disadvantage*, PSI.

Blaxter, M. (1990) *Health and Lifestyles*, Routledge.

Bouchard, T.J. Jr *et al.* (1990) 'Sources of Human Psychological Differences: the Minnesota Study of Twins Reared Apart', *Science,* 250: 223–228.

Bowlby, J. (1951). *Child Care and the Growth of Love*, Penguin.

British Red Cross, St Andrew's Ambulance Association and St. John Ambulance (2006) *First Aid Manual 8th edition*, Dorling Kindersley.

Bruner, J.S. (1997) *The Culture of Education*, Harvard University Press.

Chan, J.K. *et al.* (2006) 'Ovarian Cancer in Younger vs Older Women: A Population-based Analysis', *British Journal of Cancer*, 96(9): 1492 .

Chen, Z-Y, *et al.* (2006) 'Genetic Variant BDNF (Val66Met) Polymorphism Alters Anxiety-Related Behavior', *Science*, 314: 140–143.

Donaldson, M. (1978) *Children's Minds*, Fontana Press.

Dougherty, C.J. (1993) 'Bad Faith and Victim-blaming: The Limits of Health Promotion', *Health Care Analysis,* 1(2): 111–119.

Douglas, J. (1969) *Home and School – A Study of Ability and Attainment in the Primary School*, MacGibbon & Kee.

Ellis, A. (1957) *How To Live With A Neurotic*, Crown Publishers.

Festinger, L. (1957) *A Theory of Cognitive Dissonance*, Row Peterson.

Festinger, L. and Carlsmith, J. (1959) 'Cognitive Consequences of Forced Compliance', *Journal of Abnormal and Social Psychology,* 58: 203–210.

Flynn, J.R. (2007) *What is Intelligence? Beyond the Flynn Effect*, Cambridge University Press.

Giddens, A. (1993) *Sociology*, Polity Press.

Glanz, K., Marcus Lewis, F. and Rimer, B.K. (1997) *Theory at a Glance: A Guide for Health Promotion Practice*, National Institute of Health.

Glanz, K., Rimer, B.K. and Lewis, F.M. (2002) *Health Behavior and Health Education. Theory, Research and Practice*, Wiley & Sons.

Goffman, E. (1961) *Asylums: Essays on the Social Situation of Mental Patients and Other Inmates*, Doubleday.

Goffman, E. (1961), 'On the Characteristics of the Total Institution', cited on http://openlearn.open.ac.uk/mod/resource/view.php?id=41983

Goldfarb, W. (1947) 'Variations in Adolescent Adjustment of Institutionally Reared Children', *American Journal of Orthopsychiatry*, 17: 449–457.

Ham, C. (1992) *Health Policy in Britain: The Politics and Organisation of the National Health Service*, Macmillan.

HMSO (2001) *Valuing People: A New Strategy for Learning Disability for the 21st Century*.

Hofling, C.K. *et al.* (1966) 'An Experimental Study of Nurse–Physician Relationships', *Journal of Nervous and Mental Disease*, 141: 171–180.

Huff, D. (1991) *How to Lie with Statistics*, Penguin Business.

Jahoda, G. (1983) 'European 'Lag' in the Development of an Economic Concept: A Study in Zimbabwe', *British Journal of Developmental Psychology*, 1: 113–120.

Kotler, P. and Zaltman, G. (1971) 'Social Marketing: An Approach to Planned Social Change', *Journal of Marketing*, 35: 3–12.

MAFF (1995) *Manual of Nutrition* (10th ed.), HMSO.

Marshall, B.J. and Warren, J.R. (1984) 'Unidentified Curved Bacilli in the Stomach of Patients with Gastritis and Peptic Ulceration', *The Lancet*, 1: 1311–1315.

McGarrigle, J. and Donaldson, M. (1974) Conservation Accidents, *Cognition*, 3: 341–350.

McIntyre, S., McIver, S. and Sooman, A. (1993) 'Area, Class and Health: Should We be Focusing on Places or People?', *Journal of Social Policy*, 22(2): 213–234.

Milgram, S. (1974) *Obedience to Authority; An Experimental View*, HarperCollins.

Miller, G.A. (1956) 'The Magical Number Seven, Plus or Minus Two: Some limits on our capacity for processing information', *Psychological Review*, 63: 81–97.

Moon, J. (2001) *Reflections in Learning and Professional Development*, Routledge.

Neave, R. (1994) 'Older People' in Gough, P., Malin-Prothero, S. and Masterson, A. (eds) *Nursing and Social Policy: Care in Context*, Heinemann.

Oliver, M. (1996) *Understanding Disability: From Theory to Practice*, Macmillan Press.

ONS (2000) *Psychiatric Morbidity Among Adults Living in Private Households in Great Britain*, Palgrave Macmillan.

Parker, G. (1993) *With This Body: Caring and Disability in Marriage*, Milton Keynes Press: Open University.

Rogers, C. (1961) *On Becoming a Person: a therapist's view of psychotherapy*, London: Constable.

Russell Sage Foundation (2003) *The Promotion of Social Awareness: Powerful Lessons from the Partnership of Developmental Theory and Classroom Practice*.

Rutter, M. (1972) *Maternal Deprivation Reassessed*, Penguin.

Schaffer, H. and Emerson, P. (1964) 'The Development of Social Attachments in Infancy', *Monographs of the Society for Research in Child Development*, 29: 1–77.

Schön, D. (1983) *The Reflective Practitioner: How professionals think in action*, London: Temple Smith.

Senior, M. and Viveash, B. (1998) *Health and Illness*, Macmillan.

Smith, R. (1997) 'Gap Between Death Rates of Rich and Poor Widens', *British Medical Journal*, 314: 9.

Stonewall (2004) 'Discrimination at work – it's so over', Stonewall leaflet. Accessed at www.stonewall.org.uk/documents/stonewall_Employees_English_Final.pdf

Taylor, S. and Field, D. (1993) *The Sociology of Health and Health Care*, Blackwell Publishers.

The Home Office (2006) 'Tackling Anti-Social Behaviour, Report by the Comptroller and Auditor General', HC 99 2006–2007, 7 December.

The Stationery Office (1999) *Saving Lives: Our Healthier Nation*.

The Union of the Physically Impaired Against Segregation (1976) *Fundamental Principles of Disability*, UPIAS.

Townsend, P. (1979) *Poverty in the United Kingdom, a Survey of Household Resources and Standards of Living*, Penguin Books and Allen Lane.

Turner, J.C. (1991) *Social Influence*, Open University Press.

Walsh, M. (2004) *Introduction to Sociology for Health Carers*, Nelson Thornes.

Whitehead, M., Townsend, P. and Davidson, N. (1992) *Inequalities in Health: The Black Report and the Health Divide*, Penguin.

Woods, B. (2004) *Understanding Psychology*, Hodder & Stoughton.

Index

This index is in word by word order. Page numbers in *italics* indicate diagrams, figures and photos; page numbers in **bold** indicate information in text boxes, coloured blocks and tables.

Castle Learning Resource Centre